845

84-665

THE PILOT—Southern Pines

…MES

…RSEAS

…dnesday, October 17, 1979

Writer Rep…
…xperience

Rita Berman

Many companies in the UK have experimented with Flexitime; some have discarded the system and others continue to use it because it suits their particular work flow. It is of interest therefore to examine Rita Berman's assessment of the scheme as it affects organizations in the …nited States of America.

by Rita Berman

As the demands of homeownership and the activities of daily living become ever increasing challenges many retired people in the United States have looked for a simpler way of life. Condominiums, cluster housing and retirement villages are some of the housing arrangements which reduce living costs, offer security and minimise the responsibilities of property ownership. An increasingly popular living pattern has been the "life care" community which, in addition to housing, gives a range of medical and residential care options for its residents.

American managers, just like their British counterparts, are concerned with the problem of how to train employees quickly and efficiently. Many attend seminars or subscribe to business journals and newsletters that are specially written to help them find satisfactory answers. To a large extent, these specialty journals draw heavily on case histories of successful business operations around the country. As a writer for several such business newsletters, it is Rita Berman's job to search out successful business men or women, interview them and report on their methods of training and other areas of employee motivation, so that executives at the same administrative level may benefit from this varied exposure.

For the readers of Training, she presents a round-up selection of …he training and management methods that have been discussed …er the past few years by managers and supervisors involved : …ining employees.

Times-Outlook   October 1975

July-August 1979

The housi… …ar…t in Seattl… B… A BERMAN

The A—Z of Writing and Selling is a handbook for beginning writers, and published writers seeking to break into a new market.

"It's the kind of book I looked for, but didn't find, when I began to write," said Mrs. Berman. "I needed a how-to book that would tell me how to write and sell. I needed an easily understandable reference covering the many aspects of writing, and I wanted to know where I could find more extensive information.

"I had to read dozens of expensive books to learn the craft of writing. So, I wrote this book for the benefit of others. Here it is, my eight years of writing experience, all under one cover."

In her book Rita Berman takes you step by step through her methods for freelancing business, general interest, and hobby features. Approximately 60 sections, presented alphabetically, give the reader the inside story to almost every writing specialty. The handbook is arranged for easy access to information with subject headings and cross references, and an extensive bibliography and index.

Subjects include: advice to beginning writers, copyright laws and registration, where to get ideas, how to interview, how to query an editor, kill fees, manuscript preparation, how to avoid rejection, payment rates, tax deductions for the writer, and tips on selling.

Special expertise has been contributed by Ruth Moose on writing and selling fiction, Dennis Hensley explains how he makes multiple sales, Martha Monigle introduces you to ghostwriting, and Bette Elliott offers sound advice for those who want to syndicate a column.

the
A - Z
of
writing
and
selling

* money * fame * personal satisfaction *

by Rita Berman

Library of Congress Catalog Card Number: 81-80002
ISBN: 0-87716-117-8

For information, write Moore Publishing Company
P.O. Box 3036, Durham, NC 27705

DEDICATION

To my husband, Ezra, who encouraged me in my writing efforts by saying, "You can do it!" And to my daughters, Jessica and Rebecca, whose patience and understanding I deeply treasure.

CONTENTS

PREFACE

This handbook for beginning writers, and for published writers seeking to break into a new market, contains the basic information to help you achieve your goal. It will acquaint you with the practice of free-lancing, and point out the steps that can lead to successful sales.

When I began to write, this handbook is the kind of book I looked for but could not find. I needed a "how-to" book that would tell me how to write and sell. I needed an easily understandable reference covering the many aspects of writing. I wanted to know where to find more extensive information. Instead, I had to read dozens of expensive books to learn how to write and sell. But for you I have taken my eight years of writing and selling experience and put it all under one cover.

My entry into the writing profession began in 1971. At that time I was the owner of a secretarial service typing a novel for a client. I became a writer when I found myself writing, as well as typing, my client's book. I closed my business and became a local reporter for a weekly newspaper in Virginia.

After spending only six months with my new career my husband and I moved to Chapel Hill, North Carolina, and I had to look for an outlet for my writing all over again. I decided to try free-lancing.

What a good decision that was! Since 1972 I've sold more than 200 features, business interviews, articles, and book reviews to more than 60 magazines and newspapers in the United States and Great Britain. My work has appeared in all sorts of markets, including business and trade, general interest, professional, regional, travel, and women's interest magazines. I have been published in such diverse magazines as *Administrative Management; Architectural Design; Army, Navy, and Air Force Times Magazine; Homes Overseas; International Travel News; The Marketing Letter; Modern Business Reports; New East Magazine; Office Supervisor's Bulletin; Real Estate*

International; The Secretary; The Writer; Today's Family; Town and Country Planning Journal; and *Women's Life.*

As a professional free-lance writer I am free to choose what, and when, I write and to select my own markets. My writing is a product for sale, just like any piece of merchandise. Over the years I have learned how to concentrate my efforts towards creative marketing to find the publications that are not generally distributed on the newsstands. My list of steady sales proves the methods I use must be right.

You can be a professional writer if you do the following: work regularly and systematically; don't wait until you "feel" like writing; are curious, observant, accurate, and well-informed; are willing to interview others, to seek out the accepted authorities and those who have controversial ideas; are more concerned about communicating the message than developing a style; can face rejection slips and turn them around to your own use; study, select, and anticipate the markets for your writing; write for money, fame, or to entertain and instruct others.

The techniques of writing can be taught to anyone who wants to learn, but the drive to write, to express, is not something that is learned. The spark, the essence of creativity, must be in one's mind. Because you are spending the time to read this book, you already have this spark. This book should help you on the road to sales, whether you are a beginner who is starting or a published writer seeking to break into a new market. It is designed to help you become a professional, to inform you, and to aid your self-improvement. It is your introduction to the different fields of writing. Approximately 50 topics, giving you the inside story to almost every aspect of writing, are presented alphabetically for easy reference.

My thanks to Bette Elliott, Dennis Hensley, Martha Monigle, and Ruth Moose for their invaluable contributions to this book in their special areas of expertise. I am grateful to my husband, Ezra, for his help with the manuscript and to Sarah Shaber for her conscientious copy-editing. I would also like to thank the Dean of the School of Journalism, Richard R. Cole, and John B. Adams, Professor of Journalism, both of the University of North Carolina at Chapel Hill, for their invaluable advice and suggestions. Finally, I would like to thank the many writing friends who took time to give me their thoughts and advice in the questionnaire referred to in various sections of this book.

Adapt the advice to meet your own individual needs. I wish all my readers success in their endeavors, the thrill of publication, and the intangible rewards that come from self-expression.

Rita Berman
Chapel Hill, North Carolina
August 1980

AGENTS

A literary agent is one who sells your work for a fee. Agents in the United States deduct a 10 or 15 percent commission on all domestic sales, and up to 20 percent on foreign sales. In addition, you may be asked to reimburse the agent for such expenses as copyright fees, manuscript re-typing, machine copies, and long-distance telephone calls.

As your business representative, an agent can negotiate the sale or lease of your rights, examine contracts, suggest approval or rejection, and tell you the reasons why. An agent can examine your royalty statements, collect the monies due to you, and check on the publisher's handling of your books, keeping close watch on manufacturing details, such as the dust jacket, advertising, and publicity.

But, if you are not writing a book and you are also a beginner, do you need an agent? No, you don't; nor does the agent need you. Obviously, agents are in business to make money. They can't spend time teaching a beginner how to write saleable copy. That role is left to the writing instructor or consultant. Agents look for clients whose work can be sold on a fairly regular basis and for the highest possible fee. The writer who produces only a few articles or stories a year is a poor business prospect for an agent.

Paul R. Reynolds, a member of the Society of Authors' Representatives, reported that scarcely one-half of the professional magazine writers use an agent. "The majority of the adult book writers use an agent, but still there are many writers who do not," he said. "Most first sales to a major magazine are made by the author without benefit of an agent. Half, if not more than half, of authors' first novels and first nonfiction books are sold by the authors themselves."

If you are selling all you can write, at satisfactory rates, then you really don't need an agent. If you are a beginner, you'll soon discover where to sell your work by studying the market listings and then sending out queries. Editors will not seek you out unless they know you exist, so you have to make yourself known to them. By talking or writing to the editor directly, without the intrusion of a third party, you can quickly learn if your article or idea appeals to them. Furthermore, after you achieve a good relationship with one or more editors, you may find yourself on the receiving end of a telephone call with the editor making suggestions for articles she would like you to write. So, you can sell your work without an agent.

I enjoy the personal feedback I get from responses to queries and from readers' reactions to my published articles. By working directly with the editor, then through that contact, I can stay in closer touch with my eventual audience—the readers.

Writers of fiction are most likely to benefit from having an agent, because fiction must be written before it can be sold. With a completed manuscript in hand an agent can decide which publishers would be the most likely markets for it, and conduct the delicate negotiations that lead to obtaining the highest possible price. You can't interest publishers in an unwritten short story no matter how intriguing the plot. They want to read the completed story.

To locate an agent consult the listings of author's agents and literary services that appear in the *Writer's Handbook* and the *Writer's Market* as well as in *Literary Market Place*. Write to the Society of Authors' Representatives, Room 1707, 101 Park Avenue, New York, NY 10017 for a descriptive brochure and list of 50 agents. Be sure to send a stamped, self-addressed envelope for the reply. Another list of literary agents may be obtained from the Authors Guild, 234 West 44th Street, New York, NY 10016. Here too, it is advisable to enclose a SASE with your request.

See also Selling Your Writing

ARTICLE WRITING

Producing a magazine article involves more research and writing than a newspaper story. If you want to learn a little about a lot of subjects then magazine article-writing is for you.

"Article-writing is for those who are interested in relating today's doings to yesterday's perception so as to anticipate tomorrow's meaning," summarized Beatrice Schapper, editor of *Writing the Magazine Article.* "Magazine writing is demanding, but every day men and women, young and old, discover that editors are eager for authoritative, well-constructed, timely pieces that inform, instruct, or merely entertain," she noted.

Most editors actually prefer timely topics and good writing to a well-known author.

Magazine articles encompass a broad range of writing. A writer may produce a creative article or a factual story, a how-to piece or a profile, a behind-the-news story or a travel feature, and yet still be classified as an article writer.

The Creative Article

Some kinds of articles are easier to write and sell than others. "For the truly creative writer there is no quicker, easier, more satisfying road to paid publication than the creative article," Marjorie Holmes reported in her book *Writing the Creative Article.* Creative articles are broad in scope and therefore may be sold to a variety of markets. Holmes is an experienced practitioner of the creative article, and describes it as neither fact nor fiction, though it contains elements of both. It deals with human relationships. In the creative article ideas are more important than facts. Advice, personal experience, vigorous protest, nostalgia, humor, inspiration, or essays about some phase of life all may be described as creative articles. These subjects require almost no legwork and they are not as complicated as fiction. Some editors call these articles, "top of the head," but Holmes says she prefers to think of them as "deep of the heart."

3

Factual Articles

In contrast, the factual, how-to, profile, or the behind-the-news story, are research and reporting articles that deal in fact. These articles call for lots of legwork and headwork, usually including research at the public library, plenty of reading, first- and second-hand accounts, and interviews.

Their purpose is to inform and influence, and, on occasion, to entertain readers. To substantiate these articles the writer must offer figures, quotations, anecdotes, and insights for the reader's consideration.

Specialized Articles

These articles are not as difficult as they sound. They are merely tailored to a specific reader's interest group such as arts, dance, religion, sports, or politics. You don't need to be a specialist yourself, or to have an intimate knowledge of the subject about which you are writing. Out there is a world of experts and specialists eager to tell you about their work. All you have to do is talk to them and draw on their knowledge for readers who are interested in their subjects.

Travel Stories

If you want to write and sell travel articles let me warn you that your material must be better than the free publicity releases and syndicated material that inundate travel magazines from a variety of sources. To compete with these you will need to cover an unfamiliar area or present some fresh interesting news and facts about a familiar place. Your personal impressions may help you to sell to the travel magazines. You need to be enthusiastic and complimentary enough to cajole their readers into thinking, "Yes, that's where I'd like to go on vacation." But what if your impression of a travel resort or cruise is negative? Most travel magazines don't want to hear about it. After all, they are in business to encourage travel, not to turn readers off.

However, I do know of one outlet that wants the bad as well as the good news on travel: *International Travel News*, 2120 28th Street, Sacramento, CA 95818. Says editor David Tykol, "Don't be afraid to be honest. If a hotel or tour is rotten, say so. If good, ditto." The pay is low for submissions to Tykol's consumer-orientated magazine, but the satisfaction is high when you know your opinions are being distributed to at least 13,000 readers each month. Write for a free sample copy of the magazine and send a self-addressed stamped envelope if you wish to receive a copy of writers' guidelines. As the name implies, this is a market for international travel stories. Except for Hawaii and Alaska they do not print news about the United States.

For further reading and a look at the way eight different magazine articles were produced and sold to top-line magazines, see *Writing the Magazine Article*, by the Society of Magazine Writers, editor Beatrice Schapper. All the articles were published in the late 1960's and each author presents a case history from the time the idea for the article was conceived, through the steps of research, writing, and publication.

See also Hobby Writing

BOOK REVIEWING

> "A critic is a necessary catalyst between a creator and his audience. His comments should be helpful to the former, and informative to the latter. His function is to act as a bridge, not a barrier."
> —Sydney Harris, syndicated columnist

Book reviewing is an excellent way to break into print. The pay may be low but you'll derive a lot of satisfaction from seeing your by-line over published reviews. If you are reviwing for a local newspaper, you'll hear compliments from your readers as you go about your daily activities. When cashing a check at the local supermarket, it's nice to be told by the clerk, "Oh, you're Rita Berman, I read your book reviews."

Most newspapers don't pay for book reviews, although you do get to keep the book. The top money reported for book reviewing is at the *New York Times Book Review*, where $125 is paid for an 800 word review. *The Chicago Tribune* pays $100. Smaller papers may give you $25 to $50. Literary magazines usually only pay in copies. Some trade journals pay quite well for reviews of books pertaining to their area of business as long as the book and the review offer specific information that can be used by their readers. Such reviews are not an evaluation or recommendation of the book but an extraction of ideas attributed to the author. I've received as much as 15 cents per word for my trade journal book review.

The anticipatory excitement of opening and reading a book not yet in circulation is only equalled by unwrapping a birthday present. Both of them are full of unknown, rich delights.

I began reviewing books for the *Durham Morning Herald* after meeting a staff writer at a writers conference. I sent a follow-up letter and asked that I be put on the newspaper's list of reviewers, stating in my credits that I had already reviewed several books in the business management field.

6

Some time later, I received a couple of books to review with the instructions that I write a 500 word review, more or less, depending on how wide an interest there might be in the book. "Don't pan a book just for the sake of panning," I was told.

After I received the books I set down the following rules for reviewing. They were based on an article on book reviewing written by L.E. Sissman that appeared in *The Writer*, October 1974. I've followed them ever since.

1. Never read other reviews before you writer your own.
2. Never read the dust jacket or publisher's handout before reading and reviewing the book.
3. Never review a book you haven't read at least once.
4. Never review your own ideas instead of the author's.
5. Always give the reader a judgment and a recommendation on the book. Tell the reader what to read and what to skip.
6. Summarize the story or the argument and nothing more. But don't write a plot summary.
7. Don't give away the end of a mystery or suspense story.
8. Don't be afraid to put your own conclusions in the review. Report flaws in the work but do not be overcritical of minor errors. Do not pan without reason.

The following review, that I wrote for the *Durham Morning Herald* (April 13, 1980), is an example of how I employ these rules. My comments in parentheses will help you to dissect the review and understand the application of my rules of reviews.

FRIDERICUS. By Frederic F. Flach. Lippincott & Crowell. 254 pp. $9.95

Text of review

(Recommendation)   Run. Don't walk—to your nearest bookseller and get a copy of this book. I recommend it without reservation.

(Why)   *Fridericus*, by Frederic F. Flach, is a well-written first novel and a welcome addition to the genre of psychological suspense.

(Comparison) Flach is qualified to be ranked alongside Daphne du Maurier, Roald Dahl and John Fowles as a weaver of psychological drama. He carefully delineates the narrow line between fantasy and reality. The story held me captivated right up to the last page, and I won't forget it quickly.

(Story Line) It is about a busy New York psychiatrist, successful in his work and happy in his marriage. No fanfare of trumpets or sweeping cadenza heralds that something is about to happen to Dr. Frederic Pleier.

(Author's Writing Style) Here is an excerpt: "There are several ways in which things start to go wrong. Sometimes it happens suddenly. Life seems perfect. So you stop looking over your shoulder for trouble, and it suddenly drops on you like a girder from a construction site thirty stories up.

"More often, however, bad luck or misfortune begins in bits and pieces, little warning signals that are like the little gusts of wind, the first drops of rain that are omens of a cloudburst to come. Or it's the stillness that warns you and the crazy things that simply don't make sense."

(Action Buildup) In the case of Pleier, if there was a beginning for what happened, it was on a perfectly ordinary hot day in late August. A call regarding a patient, Matthew Holbein, the 18-year-old son of a friend, starts Pleier on a journey into the past.

(More of Plot) What he discovers about a 17th-century German physician whose name and work are similar to his own leads up to a crisis that not only imperils his sanity but his very life.

(The Reader Should Be Intrigued) The boy is convinced he is under the influence of some supernatural force. He thinks he is being pulled into some kind of void or black hole in time and has to use all his energy to fight off whatever this influence may be.

Even more disturbing is that he thinks Pleier is his father. Pleier doesn't have a son, but his namesake did.

8

(Foreboding)   The mystery deepens. A fortune teller informs Pleier that she has a vision of tears, sadness and much fear. "I see fire and many people dying, and you are trying to save them and you cannot. . . .Your life as it is now will vanish." She warns Pleier, "Your son is in terrible trouble."

(Condensation of Action)   His wife thinks he is suffering from mental fatigue. His psychiatrist warns him to "drop it." But Pleier is fascinated and frightened by the similarities between his own life and that of Fridericus Pleier in the 1600s.

Pleier finds himself slipping between the present and the past. He has experiences that cannot be explained away as nightmares.

(Treatment of Story Line)   Daringly and imaginatively, Flach tackles the subject of reincarnation and entertains the reader all the way.

(Author's Ideas)   A parapsychologist suggests that something has shifted in his life system, placing Pleier in unusually direct contact with what may have been a previous existence.

(Preparing for Climax)   Willy Gutheim proposes the possibility that Pleier might revert, in time and space, to his former self. "Something is pulling you back, some unfinished business perhaps?"

(Conclusions about the Writing)   In unraveling the mystery, the action is tight and the characters are believable. To say more would only detract from the suspense. (Withheld End From Reader)

(Author's Background)   The author, an associate clinical professor of psychiatry at Cornell University Medical College, lives in Manhattan.

Newspaper book review sections don't have the space to include an analysis of how the book could be improved. Our readers look to us for a plot synopsis and consumer guide. In other words, is the book worth buying?

As I read a book for the first time I place small slips of paper between the pages where I come across a description or passage that I may want to quote in my review. I find this is a more efficient method than jotting down page numbers and later searching for them.

I look for some points that I can praise, such as the story line. Is it different, imaginative, or is it a rehash of an overdone idea? Does the writing style make up for the poor story line? Are there well-written descriptions of places or people? If the book is a biography, why is it interesting?

When typing my review I put the title of the book, name of author, the publisher, number of pages, and price, all at the top of the page. I make a point of mentioning the title and author again in the body of the review just in case the heading is omitted from the published review.

The last paragraph in my book review is always a brief mention of the author's background, any previously published works, and whether the movie rights or book club rights have been sold. This information is almost always found on the dust jacket.

After the review is published, the book page editors sends two copies of the review to the publisher of the book. Occasionally a review elicits a response from the author. For example, six months after one of my reviews appeared I heard from one author who, although conceding that he agreed with most of my remarks, objected to the comparisons I had made between his book and another. He did not feel comparisons were fair and he may have been right. But I believe the reading public wants to know if a book is similar to, better than, or in the style of other writers of that genre. They want to know if it is worth plunking down ten dollars or more for a couple of hours reading.

How To Get Started As a Book Reviewer

Look at your hometown newspaper. Does it have a book section or an "arts" page that includes a book review? If it does, write to the arts or book section editor. If these pages are not featured in your paper, write to the general editor. Ask for permission to submit a review. If you have a particular book in mind, give the title, author, publisher, and publication date. If you have a copy of the book say so, otherwise ask if the editor has a review copy available.

Give your reasons as to why you think you'd be a good

reviewer for this book. Include samples of your published writing. If you lack publication credits, write a sample review of a book on the best-seller list and send that along instead.

Because you know that most local newspapers do not pay for reviews you do not mention payment in your query letter. However, should the editor accept your offer, publish your review, and talk about receiving more, that's the time to bring up the subject of payment. If you are refused you can then decide whether to continue to write the reviews while adding to your publication credits as well as your home library. Some writing activities pay off in intangible rewards. I believe book reviewing is one such activity. This is one case where reward comes in the form of fame, not fortune.

There are compelling reasons why a beginning writer should take on reviewing books for the local newspaper without pay. This kind of writing allows a novice to gain practice in writing under publication deadline pressure, to be forced to organize one's thinking. To learn to express this thinking in words on paper and to be able to see the appreciation of the work in a rather short time. Book reviewing can be a major contribution to building a portfolio of credits.

BUSINESS AND TRADE JOURNAL WRITING

New Stories From Old

The job of a writer in the business and trade journal field often is to write new stories from old. It's up to you to find the proper angle or slant that will provide a fresh approach to an old problem. What may appear to be ordinary material to the person you are interviewing for an article can be turned by you into an interesting piece for the reader through your insight. As a writer, you draw from your source's business skill and knowledge and assemble a story that is informative and interesting for the reader. And yet you don't need to be an expert to break into this field.

Business and trade journals are a well-paying market that too few writers know about or tackle. Pay scales for business and trade journal articles vary from two cents to fifteen cents a word. Total payment can go to $200, $300, or more for a well-documented and illustrated article in the "glossy" trade journals. The journals that I write for pay between ten and fifteen cents a word. Higher rates are given for the hard-to-get story, or a top management interview.

Some journals pay for the number of words published. That is, if you submit 1700 words and they only publish 800 you will only get paid for 800. Some pay for the number of words you send in. Still others pay a fixed sum for each article irrespective of length. So always check the market listing to see which journal offers the best rate.

What Sort of Stories Are Used?

Business and trade journals look for positive and informative success stories; stories of how people in business have found a way to do things better; whether selling a product; managing and motivating the work force; or using certain equipment. Articles for such magazines as *American Coin-Op, Candy and Snack Industry, Dental Management, Farm Building News, Florida Banker, Motor Magazine, Office Supervisors' Bulletin, Small Business Magazine*, or *Swimming*

Pool Weekly, should provide the reader with well-written ideas and suggestions on how to improve his or her business.

The titles of my business and trade journal articles give the reader an indication of what a story is all about. A sample selection follows:

"How to Use a Sales Plan to Spur Selling Efforts"...tips from the sales vice-president of a pharmaceutical company.

"Maintaining Morale During Reorganization"...the methods an organization used to retain employees and keep up production during a takeover.

"Anytime Is the Right Time for Safety"...how medical personnel at a plant used an accident-prone situation to teach the workers safety.

"How to Train Workers from Unskilled to Valuable Employees"...interview with the foreman of an instrument manufacturing company.

"Organize Yourself With a Job List"...a bank manager tells how he organizes his work load.

As you can see, the subjects of all of these articles are nothing unusual. It was the twist put into the article by the writing of it which made the interest for the reader. To write any story you must carry out some advance preparation. Learn about the topic and the company you will be describing because the depth of your preparation will be revealed in your query letter and the finished story. You don't have to become an expert, but you should know some of the jargon of the field. And you have to have your questions ready for the interviewee.

Where To Get Story Ideas

A basic knowledge of the topic you intend to tackle is a great asset in business and trade journal writing. Before I turned to writing I had spent many years as a secretary. I was familiar with office procedures and the problems that can come up in daily office life. Drawing on my own experiences, I began writing for the secretarial trade journal field. From there I progressed to writing for office training and business management journals. I read a number of books on business management techniques and talked to experts in this field, including office managers, personnel directors, and supervisors in large companies. As my knowledge of the subject increased, I was able to write and sell articles that were based on my interview with these experts.

I'm constantly on the lookout for successful individuals and businesses. Newspapers are a good source for new businesses coming into the area or people who have received awards or promotions at work. Sometimes advertisements for "help wanted" may lead me to a story. Ideas may be sparked off by browsing through the Yellow Pages of the telephone book.

Any subject in which you have an interest can be used. Like to tinker with cars? Then have a talk with your local garage mechanic. Does he have any new ideas on tune-ups, auto diagnosis, has his business volume increased recently? Find out why. This may interest *Canadian Automotive Trade Magazine*, for example, which is always on the lookout for technical, mechanical, and maintenance articles from knowledgeable sources. "Service articles can come from anywhere," they say. Length: 600 to 1400 words; pay $60 to $200.

Perhaps your interests lie in the direction of machinery and metal trade, real estate, selling, merchandising, or transportation. With more than 80 categories of business and trade journals you can select the category you prefer and then do your research by talking to people in that trade. Reading and talking about that subject will help you to gain knowledge that will later be reflected in your query letters to editors.

Where to get ideas:
* your career, hobbies, and interests
* newspapers, radio, and television
* public relations officials, personnel managers
* sales managers, purchasing managers, and so on
* company and in-house publications
* awards, promotions, and product information.

The Markets and Where to Find Them

After you get an idea for a story the next step is to find out where the market is. *The Writer's Market* lists almost 1,000 magazines in the business and trade journal field, as well as editorial needs, rates, and method of payment. Monthly magazines that give plenty of market information are *The*

Writer and *The Writer's Digest*. Both are available by mail subscription or at most bookstores and may be at your local library.

Send your material to the right market. You waste your time and the editor's, as well as incur unnecessary postage expenses, if you don't study the markets carefully and submit what the editor wants. Most journals have writers' guidelines and you can request these from the editor of the journal you are interested in. Writers' guidelines will tell you who the magazine sells to, the focus of the articles, how many articles are bought from free-lancers, whether the magazine pays on acceptance or publication, the length of article preferred, whether photographs are used, and if payment for photographs is additional.

Query the Editor

To avoid wasting time with fruitless interviews you should query the editor for whom you are interested in writing before you go out on interviews. Your aim is to tailor your work to the editor's needs and to write to sell.

Most business editors are very willing to let you know the type of articles they want and will often send along copies of their magazine for you to study as well as the writers' guidelines. They won't, however, tell you whom to interview. That's left for you to decide, as well as how much you need to research. Do sufficient reading, asking, and listening until you feel comfortable writing on the subject you've selected. Lean, accurate reporting plus intelligent interpretation of what the facts mean are strong features of business writing.

Remember, the editors of business magazines want articles that will guide their readers and will show their readers how to duplicate results in their own businesses. It is more important to provide examples of how a successful project was carried out than to quote someone on why it should be done. To put it another way, the editor and reader want to know what to do, not why to do it. That's why the personal interview with lots of illustrative quotes is so much in demand in business and trade journal circles.

In your query letter tell the editor what it is you want to write, how long a piece you plan, the names of your sources,

15

and the individuals who are going to help substantiate the story. Give an indication of when you expect to complete your story. Always send a self-addressed stamped envelope with your query letter or outline.

In response to one of my queries here's what an editor wrote to me: "What we need are well-done, fact-filled articles on how successful builders operate. We want to know how a builder succeeds and how our readers can pick up on what he is doing to also possibly succeed." Now, information like that from an editor can really put the writer on the road to a sale. You know what the editor needs and what he would like to offer his readers.

Another editor suggested, "You should ask interviewees to pinpoint current problems in supervision, discuss how they're solving these problems in their company, what results are they getting. Illustrate with examples from daily office life." This editor looks for articles that have plenty of direct quotes and a summation of the facts.

The field of business and trade journal writing is full of opportunities if you will only grab them. Editors of these journals seem to be more helpful than editors of general interest magazines in letting you know why a certain piece does not meet their needs. They may suggest ways in which you can rewrite the story to meet their requirements.

Several years ago, an outline I submitted to a New York publication was turned down because they had run a similar story a short while before my proposal was considered. Although my outline was rejected, the editor wrote to me that he wanted to enlarge his circle of writers and invited me to submit other ideas for articles. I picked up on his suggestion and since then have sold eight business interviews to him. Don't give up on a market if you get your first proposal rejected, instead try again with some other ideas.

Nor should you discard a proposal that has been turned down. Offer it to someone else. In the case of a rejected outline I mentioned above, I offered it to several other markets until I eventually placed it with a glossy business magazine that even gave me a by-line when the story was published. You should know that by-lines are not standard practice in trade journals. Some journals prefer not to let their readers know their stories come from a number of different sources. Instead they pay the writer higher rates to compensate for the lack of a by-line. However, you know you wrote the story and so does the editor and you may certainly add stories without by-lines to your list of credits.

An editor may be interested in your query but not want to offer you an assignment because it would commit him. He may, however, inform you that he will read the manuscript "on speculation." This means you take the chance that after the story has been read it might be turned down. There is no guarantee you will make a sale. Nonetheless an "on spec" story may be the way to break into a new market.

Many editors of business and trade journal magazines now insist that if they give you an assignment you must sign a "work for hire" agreement. This practice has become more common since the Copyright Act was revised and went into effect on January 1, 1978. One aspect of the revision was that work created under a "work for hire" agreement is no longer the writer's after it has been bought, but belongs to the publisher. This means that you no longer hold the reprint rights to that material and you could lose out on possible subsidiary sales. Before signing any work for hire agreements decide what rights you want to retain and then try to negotiate with the magazine.

Structured Writing

Writing for business and trade journals is usually very structured, almost conforming to a formula. There is nothing mysterious about it. Whatever tricks there are can be learned. Your task is to write an article that will guide readers and show them how to duplicate successful results in their own businesses. The task of writing these articles has three simple steps:

1. Define the problem.
2. Show what was done to solve the problem.
3. Discuss the results.

You don't have to be a business expert to sell to business and trade journal magazines, but you do need to adopt professional writing techniques. Give the editors what they want. Study their needs thoroughly. Follow through by sending manuscripts that meet those needs. No matter how long your list of writing credits, if you send an article to an editor that doesn't meet his needs, he won't buy it. However, if you can spot a new angle for a story, research it for background, interview an expert or authority for the anecdotal quotes, and then write the story up in the style that the magazine uses, then you are on your way to making a sale.

Business and trade journal writing is educational and rewarding for the writer who likes to meet people. It is a wonderful opportunity to get to know how someone else operates at work and to make money for yourself at the same time.

See also My Methods For Successful Sales
Query Letters and Outlines.

18

BUSINESS CARDS AND STATIONERY

Business cards are a useful adjunct to your business of writing. Clip them to your business correspondence to show-off your professionalism. Keep them available to pass out to contacts and to hand out at conferences, meetings, and workshops.

For my business cards, I went to a local printer and asked to see the latest designs and colors. I learned that the most popular item that he sold was a buff card with brown ink lettering. Because I wanted my card to leap out at the viewer and not look like everyone else's my choice was a rough-surfaced white card of heavier stock than the "popular" card. The lettering is in royal blue and the design is similar to that used on my stationery. I paid $24.95 for 500 cards, the minimum order the printer would take.

Give your letters a professional appearance as well by using printed stationery. This will set your letters apart from those who use the name and address typed on plain bond. If you've got a sufficiently large budget, pay a visit to your local printer and ask to see samples of style and designs. Or, you can do as I did and design your own stationery. For only $5 per hundred sheets (25% rag bond, 8 1/2 by 11 inch) I have my stationery run off at a nearby copy center. A heavier quality paper (100% rag bond) cost me only $6 per hundred sheets, a great savings over printed stationery.

This inexpensive and original letterhead was produced by using press-on letters, such as "Prestype," that are available at most stationery, art, or hobby stores. Follow the manufacturer's directions so that you get the letters lined up neatly. A unique or unusual design letterhead helps editors to remember that they've heard from you before and that's what you want. In my case, I selected a bold type-style and departed from tradition by placing my name and telephone number in capital letters across the top of the page. My address runs vertically from bottom to top on the left hand side of the paper. To use on envelopes, for my return address and to save time in typing my name and address on self-addressed envelopes, I had a large rubber stamp made in type to match my stationery. I also use this same stamp to put my name and address on any photographs I may submit with my manuscripts.

See also Typing Tips

BUSINESS EXPENSES AND RECORD-KEEPING
EQUAL TAX DEDUCTIONS

The free-lance writer can claim federal and state tax deductions for many of the expenses incurred in the course of researching, writing, and selling. However, you must be receiving payment for your literary work and conducting your writing as a business, not as a hobby. That distinction is very important.

There is a one-way tax rule for hobbies: income from a hobby is taxable; losses are not deductible. The question of whether your writing is a hobby or a sideline business arises when losses are incurred. Just as long as you show a profit, you may deduct the expenses of the activity. Your records must show that you are actively engaged in the business of writing and selling your writing. An unpublished writer may have difficulty in justifying losses year after year. According to the tax guide, *Your Income Tax*, published by the J.K. Lasser Tax Institute, if you show a profit in two or more years during a five-year period you are presumed to be in an activity for profit. However, publishing a poem or two, an article, or a short story on a sporadic basis does not meet the qualification of pursuing a business.

Records

You must substantiate your claim of being engaged in writing for profit. To do this you must keep complete and accurate books and records. In addition to the receipts for monies spent, you need an accounting of the time and effort expended in carrying out your writing. A business diary is indispensable. In it you should keep a note of your business mileage and travel expenses to interviews, writers' conferences, and seminars. Keep a note of how much time you spend in conducting the interviews or writing your articles and stories. Enter postage expenses in your diary under the date sent, include to whom sent, the title of the manuscript and the cost of the postage. Also record the date you purchase paper,

21

typewriter ribbons, envelopes, reference books and other supplies.

Save all receipts to support your tax deductions. Keep copies of correspondence, queries, manuscripts, work papers, interview notes, anything at all that will demonstrate you are actively pursuing your writing career. Earnings may be recorded on a loose-leaf list of manuscript sales or in a ledger.

I keep track of my writing production and sales in a card file and bound ledger. On 3 x 5 inch cards I enter, in chronological order, the title and to whom a manuscript was sent. The fate of the manuscripts (accepted or rejected) is noted on the card after I get a response from the editor. Flipping through these cards I can quickly learn which manuscripts need to be followed up with a letter to the editor inquiring if a decision has been made on the manuscript.

A summary of hours worked, rights sold, and earnings are recorded in my bound ledger for each individual project, as well as the date of publication and the name of the magazine or newspaper.

Tax Returns

When filing your annual income tax return fill out a Federal Schedule Form C along with the 1040 Form. On Schedule C you may deduct such expenses as automobile gasoline, oil, and other expenses or a fixed rate per mile, bank charges, business-related telephone calls from home or a pay phone, dues and publications, legal and professional fees including charges for tax preparation. Additionally, you may deduct the cost of office supplies such as stationery, pens, typewriter ribbons, photographs purchased to accompany features, or the cost of film, developing and printing; postage, writers contests and conference fees.

Schedule C also includes a section for depreciation of certain equipment or furnishings, such as typewriter, desk, chair, tape recorder, copier, answering machine, that you use for business. These may be depreciated over a number of years; they may not be taken off as a total deduction in the year of purchase.

What about the expenses of your office at home? Can these be deducted? This is a sore point with writers and others who work at home. Until a few years ago we could deduct our expenses for an office at home, but not any more. Not unless the room is used *exclusively* for your working and nothing else. If you type in it during the day and watch television in it at night you cannot claim any part of the operating expenses for that room on your income tax return.

In addition to Schedule C, if your writing or editing work nets you $400 or more in earnings, you must file a Schedule SE and pay self-employment tax, which makes you eligible for Social Security benefits. Furthermore, if you think your taxes from free-lancing will be $100 or more, you are required to pay your taxes in quarterly installments. To do this, you file a declaration of estimated tax using Form 1040-ES and mail in your estimated taxes every three months.

Consult your accountant, tax preparer, or an agent of the Internal Revenue Service for any questions you may have regarding your tax obligation. You might also ask about your eligibility for participating in either the Keogh Plan as a self-employed individual, or making tax-deductible contributions to an Individual Retirement Account in respect of any profits you make from your writing.

See also Filing System

CHECKLIST FOR PREPARATION OF BUSINESS
OR FEATURE ARTICLE

_____ Subject

_____ Possible Markets

_____ Query sent

_____ Set up interview(s)

_____ Conduct interview(s)

_____ Take photographs

_____ Transcribe notes

_____ Prepare outline

_____ Prepare rough draft

_____ Revise and rewrite draft

_____ Prepare final draft

_____ Type final draft

_____ Make copy for file

_____ Do you have a release for photographs?

_____ Make copy of release for file

_____ Caption photographs

_____ Mail off manuscript, photographs and copy of release, with self-addressed stamped envelope

_____ Enter in diary date sent with amount of postage paid

CONFERENCES, CLUBS, AND CONTESTS

If you want to meet other writers, get inside tips from the professionals, and even pick up a writing assignment or two, you should attend a writers' conference. More than one hundred conferences and seminars are held across the country each year for the purpose of supplying advice and inspiration to beginning and experienced writers.

Attending such conferences benefits you. You receive writing instruction and manuscript critiques and experience fellowship and understanding and, very important, creative stimulation.

Besides writers, agents, and editors, you will meet your potential readers at these conferences. You will find there teachers, students, librarians, book club members and many others who have reading or writing interests.

Choose your conference carefully. Listings containing the name of the conference, date(s), location, and contact name and address are usually published in *Writers' Digest*, and *The Writer* every spring. Some conferences are geared to offer the participants a variety of subjects from which to choose. The Florida Suncoast Writers Conference, one example of a larger conference, may have a half dozen different workshops proceeding at the same time with participants selecting which one they want to attend. Other conferences, such as the Tar Heel Writers Roundtable, may offer a number of lectures, one lecture at a time for the whole group to attend.

Some conferences are little more than informal get-togethers; others provide question-and-answer periods, panel discussions, manuscript critiques, and even private instruction for an additional fee. In 1980 you could have attended a wide variety of conferences: the Surfwriters Seminar for Writers, in California; the First International Conference on the Fantastic, in Florida; the New England Poets' Conference; the International Black Writers Conference; a Writing Workshop for People over 57; a Science Writers Seminar; a Travel Writing Workshop; the Womens' Writing Guild Conference; or the

Hunky Dory Writers Conference.

When you attend a conference take along any current projects just in case you decide to have a private meeting with an agent or editor about your work. Published authors are often encouraged to bring copies of their books for sale during the meeting.

Writers' Clubs

Joining a writers' club is another way of easing the "loneliness" of writing. However, to be constructive the purpose of the club should be more than just to meet and talk about problems. Find out if time is allowed for members to read portions of their work, and for the group to offer criticism and suggestions on how it might be improved. Some clubs hold a reporting session at the beginning of each meeting, when members report on sales, assignments, or encouragement they may have received from editors since the last meeting.

If there isn't a club in your area why not start one yourself? Even a group of four or five can help each other with encouragement, manuscript criticism, and marketing advice. For more information send 50 cents to *Writer's Digest* and ask for Chet Cunningham's reprint, "How To Start/Run a Writer's Club."

Once you've made some sales there are a number of professional organizations you can join. The National Writers Club, is a non-profit organization whose purpose is to assist and serve the free-lance writers. This organization provides help, guidance, manuscript criticism, and moral support to its members through the mail. It also acts on behalf of all writers, constantly striving to improve writing standards, upgrade the rates authors receive, and to improve the methods of payment. If you are trying to get a delinquent publisher to pay up you can relate your problem to the NWC and they will assist you by contacting the publisher on your behalf. For further information contact Donald E. Bower, The National Writers Club, 1450 South Havana, Suite 620, Aurora, CO 80012.

In addition to the National Writers Club, I also belong to the professional organization of Women in Communications, Inc. WICI was founded more than 70 years ago and has

26

approximately 9,000 members in 165 chapters. Membership is open to women and men in all fields of communications whose careers require communications skills and creativity. The purposes of the organization are: to work for a free and responsible press; to unite women communicators and recognize their distinguished achievements; to maintain high professional standards; and to encourage members to greater individual effort. Contact the national office, Women in Communications, Inc., P.O. Box 9561, Austin, TX 78766 for more information.

More than 40 professional organizations are listed in the 1980 edition of the *Writer's Market.* By joining a professional organization you gain access to specialized information and sources of market and job information that might not otherwise be readily available.

Contests

Most writers reap their rewards in the form of publication, payment, and the occasional complimentary letter, months after they have written a story or article. Winning a contest is another way of achieving recognition. In 1973 I entered my first contest by sending an unpublished mansucript to the Article Writing contest of the Tar Heel Writers Roundtable. I was primarily attending the Roundtable as a participant but had also obtained an assignment to cover the Roundtable for a local newspaper. You can imagine my surprise when I learned that I was one of the winners. That First Place Award and a silver trophy inspired me to greater writing efforts. One year later I was back at the Roundtable, only this time I was a member of the faculty.

I try to enter at least one writing contest each year, not only to sharpen my skills and see how my manuscripts compare with others, but because the publicity that accrues from even an Honorable Mention may lead to a writing assignment. It most certainly produces recognition at the local level, and local fame is a strong impetus to more and better work.

COPYRIGHT LAW AND REGISTRATION PROCEDURE

What is a copyright? It is the right, accorded by law, to prohibit the unauthorized copying of original works of literature, art, music, and other works of creation. The right belongs to the author or to someone to whom the author has transferred this right.

As author and copyright owner, therefore, you hold exclusive rights to reproduction, adaptation, publication, performance, and display of the work. However, in the case of a work made for hire (unless there is written agreement to the contrary) the person for whom the work was prepared is considered the author and thus owns all rights comprised in the copyright. This rule also applies to work written for a newspaper or magazine during a period of employment as a staff writer.

Under the new copyright statute (Title 17 of the United States Code, dated January 1, 1978) there is now a single system of statutory protection for all copyrightable works, whether published or unpublished.

Duration of Copyrights

For works created after January 1, 1978, the term of protection starts at the moment of creation and lasts for the author's lifetime, plus an additional 50 years after the author's death.

For works made for hire and for anonymous and pseudonymous works (unless the author's identity is revealed in Copyright Office records), the duration of copyright is 75 years from publication or 100 years from creation, whichever is shorter.

Published copies of a work should bear a copyright notice, but omission or errors will not immediately result in forfeiture of the copyright and can be corrected within certain time limits.

28

Copyright Registration System

The classification system for copyright registration has been simplified in that there are now only five categories instead of the fifteen provided for under the old law. Application forms have been revised to correspond with these new registration categories. The categories that concern writers are Class TX (Nondramatic Literary Works) and Class PA (Works of the Performing Arts).

The Class TX category includes all types of published and unpublished works written in words (or other verbal or numerical symbols). Fiction, nonfiction, poetry, periodicals, textbooks, reference works, directories, catalogs, advertising copy, and compilations of information, should be registered under this classification.

Class PA is appropriate for registering published and unpublished works prepared for the purpose of being "performed" directly before an audience or indirectly "by means of any device or process." Musical works, including any accompanying words; dramatic works, including any accompanying music; pantomimes and choreographic works; and motion picture and other audiovisual work should be registered under this classification.

If your work contains copyrightable material falling into two or more classes, you should choose the one class that is most appropriate for the work as a whole. In the case of a contribution to a periodical, the proper class would depend on the nature of the contribution, not of the larger work in which it appears. A cartoon, published in a newspaper, for example, would be registered in Class VA for visual arts whereas a newspaper would be registered under Class TX.

It is not necessary to file a separate registration for each individual article or story that you have had published. For a single fee, you may register your claim for a collective copyright to cover all original contributions to periodicals and newspapers during a 12-month period, recommends Don Glassman, author of *Writers' and Artists' Rights.* For example, a collection of newspaper columns that you are self-syndicating may also be registered on a single application and fee, if the items are all submitted as a single unit. Contact the Register of Copyrights, Washington, D.C., for additional regulations dealing with this subject.

29

Requirements for Deposit and Registration of Copies

The deposit of copies for purpose of making a copyright registration and the deposit of copies for the Library of Congress calls for two separate actions. (The old copyright law, prior to January 1, 1978, combined deposit and registration into a single requirement.)

Deposit for copyright registration is voluntary. It is not a condition of copyright protection but is a prerequisite to an infringement suit. Subject to certain exceptions the remedies of statutory damages and attorney's fees are not available for infringements occurring before registration. Registration for both published and unpublished works can be made at any time during the copyright term by depositing the necessary number of copies with an application fee.

Deposit for the Library of Congress

In general, the owner of copyright, or the owner of the right of first publication in the work, has a legal obligation to deposit, in the Copyright Office, two copies for the use of the Library of Congress. This is a mandatory requirement. Failure to make the deposit can give rise to fines and other penalties but it does not affect copyright protection.

Use of Mandatory Deposit to Satisfy Registration Requirement

The two separate actions of registration and deposit can be combined into one, to satisfy both the deposit requirements for the Library of Congress and the copyright registration requirements, if the copies are accompanied either by an application for copyright registration and fee, or by a letter requesting that they be held for connection with a separately forwarded application. (Write to the Copyright Office for further information.)

Application Forms for Copyright Registration

All forms are supplied free of charge by the Copyright Office upon request. The basic copyright application form is a single sheet with spaces to be completed on the front and back. Certificates of registration are issued after the Copyright Office has added the registration number and effective date of

30

registration to the application. The application is then reproduced on a preprinted and signed certificate form, the official
seal is embossed onto the certificate, which is then mailed to
the applicant. The numbered applications are filed as the
official record of the registration.

Fees For Registration and Other Services

Registration of Copyright Claims, for each registration including a certificate bearing the Copyright Office Seal	$10.00
Renewals	$ 6.00
Recordation of Documents, Basic Fee, for the recordation of a transfer of copyright ownership or other document of six pages or less listing no more than one title	$10.00
Additional Pages or Titles, for each page over six and each title over one	$ .50
Additional Certified Copy of the record of registration	$ 4.00
Other Certifications including certifications of photocopies of Copyright Office records	$ 4.00
Searches, including Report, hourly fee for each hour or fraction spent by the staff of the Copyright Office in searching the official records and for the making and reporting of a search	$10.00

NOTE: Searches are not made (and are not necessary
under the copyright law) to determine whether a similar work
has already been copyrighted.

All remittances should be sent in the form of a check,
money order, or bank draft, payable to Register of Copyrights.

For a copy of the complete statute, Public Law 94-553,
write to the Copyright Office, Library of Congress, Washington, DC 20559. Some of the information provided in this
section was excerpted from the following circulars that are
available from the Copyright Office

Application Forms, Circular R1d

Classification System of Copyright Registration,
    Circular R1c

Copyright Fees, Circular R4
Deposit for Library of Congress, Circular R7A
Fair Use, Circular R21
Highlights of the new Statute, Circular R99
Works Copyrighted before January 1, 1978,
   Circular R15a

See also Legal Information for Writers
Rights for Sale

DISCIPLINE

If you want to become a writer you must be a self-starter and establish good writing habits to help you work regularly and systematically. To be a writer, instead of a "would-be" writer, calls for discipline and the ability to put aside other tasks in favor of the act of writing. It's not an easy job. It is boring and physically tiring at times, yet the tedium is quickly dispelled by the exhilaration that comes from creating a poem or weaving a story that you know to be good. Even the writing and assembling of a nonfiction article can be satisfying when your rough ideas get worked into shape and you see your personal interpretations emerge.

The primary obstacle that a beginning writer encounters is the matter of discipline, wrote novelist Borden Deal. According to Deal, discipline is a continuing concern, no matter how long or successfully you write. "After twenty years of full-time writing I still have that moment of revulsion every day when I sit down at the typewriter to go to work," he said.

Write every day, suggested Deal. "An hour, two hours is all that is necessary." Deal's advice has merit, because in order to refine and polish your writing skills you need constant application. Like many other skills, writing needs practice over and over again in order to produce improvement. The actual amount of time you spend is less important than the frequency or regularity with which you do it. Don't expect to make much progress if you spend only an afternoon writing, say, once every three months. If you can't manage every day what about writing every other day? Or once a week? Even five pages a week can mount up. At that rate, by the end of a year you would complete 250 pages, the equivalent of a book.

It should be obvious why a regular writing routine is essential. If you sit back and wait until the writing mood strikes it may never come. Alternatively, the mood may descend upon you but arrive at an inappropriate time when you are not free to respond. Therefore, it is best to set up a writing situation where you cajole the words to come out.

Those who intend to be writers should ignore the chatter about mood and inspiration; instead set up some daily routine and stick to it, says Hayes B. Jacobs in *Writing and Selling Non-Fiction*. "Get into the writer's harness. Until you do, your chances of realizing any substantial psychological or monetary reward from your writing will remain slight."

Establish a realistic writing routine that can fit in with your other activities so you can stick to it. Don't set up a routine that is impossible to follow, because you'll only end up frustrated and unhappy, and that will affect your writing. It took me years to accept the fact that my family responsibilities prevented me from writing as frequently as I would like during the summer months. Having accepted this fact, I now make a big push in May and June, coast along in July and August, and then resume again with great enthusiasm in September.

Shut Out The World

Experience has taught me that writing letters to friends, making telephone calls, or any socializing with other people during the time I am working on an assignment only depletes the amount of creative energy I have. So, I have become ruthless! When I get involved with a story I shut myself off from my friends. They know I'll surface again when the pressure is off. To a certain extent I try to shut myself off from family too. I may be physically present but my mind is grappling with other things. This problem of the need for isolation is not unique. "It's what you have to do to yourself and to your family just in order to write. You must instruct your family to stay away from you, not to come near you, not to speak to you," is the way Frank Mankiewicz puts it.

Along with the need for isolation I find I need a certain special place to write. My thoughts seem to know that once I am sitting at my desk it is all right for them to come out. I dry up if I try to write in a different location. Other writers have this need for a special place, a writing situation. In an interview with Arthur F. Gonzalez, Jr., in *1978 Writer's Yearbook*, author Frederick Forsyth said that he works best in a small working area, always facing the wall.

Stick To It

"Don't sit down and try to think desperately of something to write. . . .The two hours a day, or one hour a day, whatever it is. . .that is the time to work, to turn the idea into the reality of words. Always have in your mind a backlog of things you want to work on," said Deal.

I try to work three or four hours a day without pause. To help maintain my writing production, I make a list of future projects and set deadlines for completion of each one. New ideas get added at the bottom of the list as they crop up, and I check off the ones that are completed. Once a month I type up a new list. By comparing the new list with the old I can quickly see how much progress I have made. In turn this spurs me to greater efforts.

Success does not come overnight. As Deal put it, ". . .the writer must take the long view. You must be patient, and diligent, and you must know that it is in you to write good stuff in a good way that will merit the time and attention of a reader. . .you must have implicit faith in that potential."

See also You Set the Pace

EDITORS' RESPONSES

What are the responses you may get from a query to an editor? Most responses produce the following categories of statements:

1. not interested.
2. already published a similar story.
3. overstocked.
4. interested on speculation.
5. offers assignment.

If an editor responds to a query with "no interest" in your article and you feel that your article is still worthwhile, quickly find another potential market to query. Don't sulk about the lack of interest; it may have nothing to do with the quality of the article, but more with a wrong choice of market.

A response like "already published" can be an excellent clue that you do have a good idea. Magazines often play follow-the-leader and you can take advantage of this if the market has not been saturated. By querying similar markets you may be able to turn a refusal into a published article. If the market has been saturated by similar ideas, remember that these spurts can be seasonal and a 6-or 12-month wait can be rewarding.

When an editor declines because of overstocking, query another market. If you haven't sold your idea within a year, then send a second query to the first editor who turned you down because of overstocking. It's quite possible that his inventory may now be depleted sufficiently to permit buying new stories.

An "interested on speculation" response is a good sign and indicates that your story has enough appeal to warrant a reading. You have to take the chance that after it is submitted it may be turned down. There is no guarantee that you will make the sale.

After you submit a story on speculation you may hear

from the editor: "We'd like to use it next summer (or winter). Please let us know if it would be all right to hold your story and photos until then." In this situation you have the choice of agreeing to the magazine holding your story or asking for the return of your submission so you can submit it to a different market.

I once replied to a "hold for later" letter that I was agreeable to having the story and photographs held for later publication provided they were conidered "accepted for publication and pay, and were no longer on speculation."

Supposing you send in a story on speculation and the editor informs you that it needs rewriting before he will decide whether to buy it or not. What is your reaction? Don't be indignant. Re-read the letter for clues as to how you can improve the story in order to better meet the editor's needs.

An experience like this happened to me in 1974 when an editor rejected a real estate story submitted on speculation but informed me that it was really two articles in one. One was about a real estate company and the other about how I successfully sold my own home. "We were much more interested in the latter, but it didn't have enough 'meat' on it to justify giving feature treatment," he informed me. "If you would care to try again and give us a detailed, factual article on the trials and tribulations and vice versa of selling your own home, please do."

I took his advice and rewrote along the lines he suggested. I mailed the revised version some three weeks later and his enthusiastic reply more than repaid the extra time spent on the story. "Your rewrite of the How to Sell Your Home article came as a pleasant surprise. I find it acceptable and we will run it." Reading between the lines of his reply I assumed that too few writers bother to rewrite after they have been rejected with suggestions.

Even if your "on speculation" article is rejected outright, the editor may like your writing style and propose a more favorable idea. Another editor wrote to me "...we publish articles related more to home decorating and gardening rather than maintenance. If you have any articles to submit in these two areas, I'd be happy to look at them."

Any dialogue you can enter into with an editor can help

you in future sales. He may even suggest another market. A rejection letter to me from one editor read, "Your manuscript is well-written but unfortunately it does not fit our editorial requirements. If you haven't already done so, you may want to submit this to ----------- in -----------. It would fit their publishing nicely, I believe."

The response we'd all prefer to get reads something like the delightful acceptance letter one overseas editor sent to me. It went as follows: "I like your report on 'Training Activity in the USA' very much. It is racy, factual and slickly written and I am as a result publishing it in the August/September edition of *Training* magazine. . . .I would be interested in other articles on specific training ideas, techniques, or courses no matter how crazy or pie-in-sky or even downright sensible."

The most welcome response to a query letter is one that offers you an assignment. Because I've made enough contacts in my years of writing and selling to be able to get assignments for my work I now rarely write on speculation. However, submitting on speculation is an excellent way for a beginner to break in, or for a published writer to get into a new field. On speculation pieces give you the opportunity to prove you are worthy of an assignment. After you've written two or three pieces for the same magazine and you know they like what you are doing because they are publishing your writing, you are in a better position to bargain for higher pay and for more assignments.

After you receive an assignment from an editor you should confirm in writing that you accept the assignment and indicate when you anticipate completing it. This action is more than a courtesy towards the editor; it establishes a contract between you and the editor. If by chance you find yourself so busy that you cannot complete the assignment within a reasonable time, do let the editor know.

An assignment gives you encouragement that your idea for an article has merit. Researching a story on assignment is less formidable than when you are working on speculation. An assignment confers upon the writer a special authority. You can expect a more positive reply when requesting an interview on the basis that such-and-such magazine wants to know what your interviewee is thinking. For the interviewee, this situation can be especially flattering, and you will get a more open interview. You are no longer working in the dark. When offering an assignment the editor may make suggestions as to length and treatment of the article and the points that should be included. By following these suggestions you can be more confident that your article will be published.

In the event that it isn't published you should be paid a "kill fee." Offering a kill fee in addition to the assignment is the closest thing to a firm commitment that an editor ever makes to a freelance writer.

See also Kill Fees

FICTION: THE STORY OF A SHORT STORY

(c) 1980 by Ruth Moose

(This section has been contributed by Ruth Moose. Ruth lives in Albemarle, North Carolina, edits a literary magazine, the *Uwharrie Review* teaches Poetry in the Schools, and is a columnist for the *Charlotte News*. Her nonfiction pieces have appeared in the *New York Times*, *Newsday*, *Atlanta Journal*, and *Woman's Day* to cite only a few. Her short stories have been published in *Atlantic Monthly*, *Good Housekeeping*, *Ohio Review*, and *SC Review*.)

Somerset Maugham said there was a short story on every street corner. I found one at the K-Mart. All you have to do is to be there with your mind furrowed, let the seed sift in, know when to water and where to weed.

It's easy to identify thistles from wheat, but what can grow in a short story? Different seeds grow for different folks. And every story is different. The story I mentioned above began with a single line of dialogue. It could just as easily have begun with seeing a woman stand with umbrella in hand, stop and stare at the top window in a vacant home. Or on a trip with my father-in-law to buy a cow for his farm; letting the details of that barn, that itinerate preacher-cow trader who was trying to foster off on us a one-eyed cow, sink into my mind. Or searching back within myself to the first time I ever really knew I was alive. Not the stories my mother had told me of childhood things, but my own first private memory of awareness of existence. Or an object like my grandmother's wedding ring and the story of an unusual marriage.

Whatever turns your gears that turns facts into gold. For me fiction usually begins with a tiny fact, rooted in reality. From there, like the Miller's Daughter in the fairy tale, I must spin and spin until an end appears. (If there is a Rumpelstilt-skin, he's the muse at my elbow rudely jumping up and down demanding to know what happens next? And is that logical? Are you sure you know what you're doing? Until finally a character pushes him out of the way and tells me the story.)

With fiction you don't always know if you're spinning straw into gold. It could turn into silk, or gossamer. . .or a rope you think might be a relief to lower down and leave the tower you have locked yourself into. And while you're dangling from that rope, you can enjoy the view, look at the green world below. If you're patient enough and don't rush things, you can land on your feet.

The story I found at K-Mart began with something one of the aqua-smocked check-out girls said to another. From her register, she glanced out the plate glass window to the darkened parking lot beyond and said, "He's still out there."

Her sentence, something of her tone of voice, landed on my head like a leaping cat. And clung. I stroked it all the way home, played ball with it back and forth. Who was still out there? Was she or was she not looking forward to meeting him after work. I decided the latter since the idea contained more suspense. Did her voice have a tinge of fear, or did I imagine it?

Sometime between that 10 PM closing time and the next day at my desk, I wrote the line of dialogue down. Now to weave the story around it, or pull it from a story line like a strand of yarn from a skein, allowing for knots and tangles along the way.

I had characters. Gave them names. (I keep a written list in a pink indexed notebook.) I knew their occupations, but where did they live? How did they spend off hours? Beryl, the prettier one, I decided, lived on the top floor of an older house owned by a nosey landlady. She had shared her apartment with "Knotty," the boy in the parking lot. Their relationship had been broken off. Was she sorry? Did she want him back? I wrote the story to find out. Even then I didn't know. In my first version Beryl ended up raising a window and yelling out to him in the night, in case he had followed her home. Challenging him. We don't know if he responded.

I read the story to a workshop group I've met with once a month for the past ten years. A good friend and good writer didn't like my end. She maintained Beryl would respond in a different way.

Sometimes I can see and use a suggestion. This time I didn't. I mailed it out. Because the story was not about a moon-June and roses relationship, but had a sinister element about it, I knew none of the slick women's magazines would be interested. It was a rather off-beat story. I sent it to *Redbook* which leans a little sometimes toward the literary story.

My story, which I had titled "Out There," came back in eight weeks with a letter from the editor saying while they liked the situation, they didn't like the treatment.

I began the rounds of literary magazines. *Prairie Schooner.* I had published there before. *Southwest Review.* I wanted to publish there. The story kept coming back like a homing pigeon. I kept sailing it around. Two years went by. I saw an announcement of a new publication, *Southern California Review.* Reasoning they wouldn't be overstocked or backlogged or some of those other words that appear regularly in rejection material, I sent them the story.

Bingo, by return mail, *Southern California Review* accepted. . .if I'd revise the ending. My friend had been right. I wrote her so and revised my story. It was easier with some distance from the material. I simply "re-thought" the character and situation of Beryl, her lonelines and the fact that "Knotty's" absence had changed her. If he came back she would be different and he might not find easy acceptance. But I left the reader wondering if "Knotty," out there, does return. And I changed the title to the obvious, "Knotty." "Out There" had a ring of outer space or science fiction to it. Didn't fit the story.

A word here about titles. They should grab your reader. And are more important than most writers think. This is your first impression on an editor. You want their interest. Titling takes thinking. . .and time. Go through a short story anthology and read titles. Roll them on your tongue. Think of your favorite ones. I like Flannery O'Connor's "A Good Man is Hard to Find" or an early Robert Penn Warren, "The Patented Gate and the Mean Hamburger," or Katherine Anne Porter's "Noon Wine." I'm proud of some of my titles. Some came fast and easy, others through a time and error process.

My story about the itinerate preacher was called, "The Angel of the Lord and the One-Eyed Cow." The story of my grandmother's wedding ring, "The Saturday Evening Post Every Sunday Morning." The story of my first memory, "To Banbury Cross." A story published in the May 1980 issue of *Tar Heel* magazine was called, "The Vanilla Man." No other title could work as well. The story I published in *Atlantic Monthly* (September 1978) was called "A Biography in Seven Lives," a womans' story. I like to think my titles lead readers (and editors) into the stories.

Six months later the story was published. I received author's copies of *Southern California Review* and a letter. The magazine was to be discontinued after one issue. Good work was too hard to find.

I mourned the loss of a short story market. Good markets are hard to find. . .literary or slick. Especially for short stories. It's sad that more people write short stories than read them. In golden days, when the short story was king (or at least head jester in the marketplace), weekly magazines paid top money for fiction. They ran ten or twelve stories per issue, fifty-two issues a year. Plus novellas. . .an almost forgotten art form. Check old magazines in antique shops. They were fiction filled. Women's magazines ran thirteen to fifteen short stories, beautifully illustrated, in each issue. Fiction writers were featured on the covers. Today it's either the President's lady, or ex-President's ladies, or mamas, or articles on diet, sex or divorce. Some issues appear fictionless. They're like "bread" sandwiches.

Those who love fiction and the short story form, who read and write it, should lodge some response. As we should compliment when a magazine runs an especially well done piece of fiction. The fiction editor of a popular women's magazine that receives 40,000 pieces of unsolicited material a year, and buys maybe a dozen, said she rarely gets any response to the stories she runs. She would welcome comments.

Marketing, and that includes attending seminars where editors speak, and reading, reading, reading, is seventy-five percent of writing. You can spend much more time selling a short story than it took to write it. Expect this. I had a story in a recent issue of *Tar Heel* magazine, the story had been written ten years before. The story I published in *Atlantic* was sent out seventeen times. (It was also revised five times.) A story I sold to *Good Housekeeping* was on the first voyage out. A rarity, I assure you.

I start every class in creative writing by putting a definition for talent on the board. "Talent is long patience." (I didn't originate this, but selected it from somewhere because it's the best definition I've ever found.) Sometimes I feel I should have it tattooed on my brain, or at least my typewriter. Long patience. . .in writing, revising, marketing and reaching readers. But it does happen. Believe in that.

FILING SYSTEM FOR WRITERS

"How do you keep your writing materials organized?", I was asked at the Tar Heel Writers Roundtable some years ago. "Just like I did when I was a secretary," I replied. "I use a filing system. Writers should be like any other business people when it comes to handling basic paper work."

Remove that pile of papers from your desk and put them into a filing system that will help you to operate more efficiently! The pile of papers may give to someone else an impression of great productivity on your part. But more often than not disorganization will lower your writing production because of the time spent in searching frantically through the pile for a particular note or reference.

Records of manuscripts, correspondence, queries, research material, interview notes, and ideas for future stories must be easily accessible if they are to help, not hinder, your productivity. Furthermore, records of business expenses must be kept in order to justify your tax deduction claims.

I converted the bottom drawer of my desk into a hanging file by using a Pendaflex$^{(R)}$ kit that I bought at an office supply store. The Pendaflex$^{(R)}$ frames come in six sizes and are adjustable to most drawer lengths. Folders are placed on the frame rails and slide easily so that you can reach the folders at the back of the drawer as quickly as those in the front. To identify the contents of each folder, plastic tabs may be inserted wherever you want at the top of the folder. I divided the folders in my file into five sections by lining up the tab headings in each section.

My desk drawer file contains future and current projects, arranged so that as the idea nears publication it proceeds to the back of the file. Correspondence with editors and query letters are kept in the front. The second section holds "Future Projects" that I am seriously contemplating writing. The third section holds "Work in Progress." A separate folder for each idea or interview is kept in this section. The fourth section is used for manuscripts that have been sent out and are "Waiting for Word from Editors." The fifth and last section of this drawer contains "Manuscripts in Press."

After publication I file one copy of each article chronologically in a three-ring binder, one binder for each calendar year. Another set of binders contains duplicate tear sheets of published stories, this time cross-filed by topic. This is very helpful for quickly locating copies of published stories that I may wish to send along with a query letter on the same or a . similar subject.

A separate three-drawer file contains data already used for published stories, notes on ideas and research material for future articles, and tax records and receipts. Data already used for published stories, such as correspondence with editors, notes, and interview transcriptions are kept in separate folders, identified by the subject or interviewee's name, and filed alphabetically.

Research materials for future articles that are only at the idea stage (such as newspaper clippings, notes, and corre spondence) are filed alphabetically under headings such as Animals, Education, Management, Real Estate, Secretarial, etc. Organizing and maintaining up-to-date records takes a little time but I believe it helps me to make more sales. When I see there is sufficient information in my ideas-file to write an article on a specific subject I then transfer that folder into the desk drawer and start querying editors for their interest.

See also Business Expense and Record-Keeping
Equal Tax Deductions

FOREIGN SALES

Do not overlook the foreign magazine market because they can open a second market for a writer's work. Quite a large number of foreign magazines will consider purchasing material previously published in the United States or Canada and will buy it for first publication in their country.

When I first began free-lancing I submitted my stories to the local and regional markets. Later I found I could sell these same stories to overseas markets. Here's how I sold to an English magazine and became its American correspondent with an ongoing assignment to report anything I found of interest on the secretarial and office scene.

I had received my secretarial training at Pitman's Business College in England. After I switched my career to that of writer, I wrote to the head office of Pitman's in London enclosing an article I had written and sold to the American market. I suggested it might be of interest to their students. The topic was how my secretarial training had helped me as a writer. I also enclosed a list of writing credits, my publicity photograph, and a self-addressed envelope with an international reply coupon attached.

Two weeks later the editor thanked me for the manuscript and photograph and asked permission to use it in the *MEMO* magazine. She told me the rate of payment was about three cents per word (at the then current exchange rates) and would be made on publication.

I quickly acknowledged my satisfaction with the payment rate and asked for two copies of the published edition. Remember, I had already sold this story to the American market and all I had done was retype my manuscript and mail it out. Any money I then received from foreign or reprint sales was almost all additional income. In my acceptance letter I suggested another topic for a feature and queried the editor's interest. Almost by return of mail she replied, "send it to us." And thus I became her "American correspondent," producing a string of more than a dozen articles on secretarial and office topics until policy changes by the magazine's executive staff resulted in a reduction and eventual elimination of American features.

By that time, however, I was writing regularly on housing and real estate topics for another British magazine. Here, too, I broke into the market with a story that had already been sold to a regional American housing magazine. In accepting my first submission the editor wrote, "I hope that we shall be able to accept further articles from you in due course as we always welcome ideas." I followed up with several proposals and now have another market that will take everything I can write for them.

Some of my housing features are written with the English market in mind and are then later sold to American publications. Occasionally, if the story is very timely, I will prepare it first for the American market. Either way, the second sale calls for very little additional effort and more than repays for the time and postage used.

Foreign magazines generally pay less than American publications. Rates for articles mostly fall into the $20 to $200 range.

Sources for foreign markets may be found in the reference section at your public library. See Ulrich's *International Periodicals Directory*, published by R. R. Bowker & Company, New York.

I have found the directory, *The Writers' and Artists' Year Book*, published annually by Adam and Charles Black, 35 Bedford Row, London, WC1, England, to be very useful. It includes journals and magazines published in Great Britain, South Africa, Australia, Canada, East and Central Africa, India, New Zealand, and Africa, as well as information on syndicates, news, and press agencies.

Sending Manuscripts Overseas

I send my overseas queries and manuscripts by air-mail. It takes only a week or so compared to a month or more by surface or sea-mail. For queries I use the single sheet air-letter forms that can be obtained from the Post Office.

The editors of magazines to which I contribute regularly pay the postage on all return correspondence so I do not have to send International Reply Postal Coupons. When submitting manuscripts to foreign markets without an agreement with the editor to pay for return postage, include International Reply Postal Coupons instead of the customary self-addressed stamped envelopes. U.S. stamps are not valid for postage from foreign countries. An International Reply Coupon is exchangeable in any other country for stamps representing the international postage on a single-rate, surface-mail letter.

For information on overseas mail rates ask at your local post office or write to International Mail Classification Division, U.S. Postal Service, Washington, DC 20260 and ask for the free booklet, "International Postage Rates and Fees."

See also Rights for Sale
Selling Your Work

FORMULA FOR FEATURES

Feature stories call for topics that are timeless and of interest to readers no matter when the story is read. Unlike the inverted pyramid news story, which can be cut at any point, the feature article has a conclusion in addition to its lead and body.

A strong lead is crucial in feature writing to draw the reader into the story. Immediately after the lead you must sustain that reader interest by providing the reason or justification for your lead remarks. This section is sometimes referred to as the bridge, hook, angle, or peg of the story. The next step is to prove your point by using illustrative anecdotes or factual substantiations. Keep the direction of the feature story flowing upward towards its conclusion. A strong closing paragraph should balance the hard-hitting lead. In this final paragraph you might summarize the points you have covered earlier, or restate the lead in different words.

An excellent example of how to use this formula for feature writing appears in Robert C. Ruark's novel, *The Honey Badger.* Alec Barr, the hero of the book, told how he switched from newspaper writing to magazine features and failed to make sales until a friendly editor gave him a diagram formula showing how it could be done.

A magazine piece has just as much of an architectural form as a building or any other precise structure, the editor explained to Barr. The anatomy of a magazine article begins with an opening anecdote that should set the scene and mood and be most indicative of the character of the piece, whether it is about a person or a thing. A matching anecdote, placed at the end, complements the opening and gets you out of the piece in the same mood.

Your customer-grabber should come in just behind your opening anecdote and is your sales pitch to the reader. "Here is where you demand that he read the piece; here is your personal guarantee of why he must waste an hour reading the piece. The sentences should be short, punchy, and indisputably true," wrote Ruark.

He explained that every time you make a flat statement, you've got to bolster it with either a short anecdote or at least a statistic. "If you say a man's a good horse trainer, you have to come in behind with the statement that his nags had ten firsts, twenty seconds, and thirty thirds out of 65 starts last year—like that. Fact or fiction, your reader's got to believe you," concluded the editor.

Before writing your feature, organize your thoughts and material. Establish ahead of time what you want your article to say. But don't expect to keep it all in your head. An outline will help to keep track of what you want to write. And, if for any reason you have to put aside your writing project, you can easily pick up the threads again by referring to the outline.

I use the "HEY YOU SEE SO" method of outlining suggested by Walter S. Campbell some thirty years ago in his book *Writing: Advice and Devices.* (See table below.) Campbell's HEY is the same as Ruark's "customer-grabber." It pulls the reader and gets them involved in the story. The YOU holds the interest while SEE concentrates upon the facts. Finally, SO is the end of the piece, the summing-up or conclusion.

Campbell's method works well for how-to or informative features, as well as informal essays.

Features Formula

Structure	Campbell Method	Ruark Method
Lead	HEY	Customer-grabber
Justification	YOU	Reason
Evidence to prove points suggested	SEE	Illustrative anecdotes, facts, statistics, to bolster your statements
Final paragraph wrap-up	SO	Matching anecdotes to complement opening. Get reader out of piece satisfied.

1. Prepare an outline by making a list of words, phrases, or sentences to remind you of all the items and points you've thought of and wish to cover in your feature. Go over these rough notes and decide what the order should be.
2. Establish the points that can serve as main divisions or evidence in SEE.
3. From these points decide what kind of HEY you should use to attract the reader.
4. What kind of YOU to hold interest.
5. What will you use for the wrap-up or conclusion. (SO)

Do not try to write any of the sections in final form at this stage. The outline should be used as a guide to prompt the flowing of your thoughts and to keep you moving in the right direction. Once you have a rough draft down on paper you will be in a better position to see if the feature has strength from beginning to end. Prune away the weak spots and revise and rewrite where needed.

With the aid of an outline you can prevent overwriting and save time. Newspaper reporters and many professional free-lance writers are frequently given assignments to produce their stories with only a specific number of words. For example, an editor may respond that she likes your query but only wants to see 1500 words on the topic. It doesn't make sense for you to research and write 3000 words on the subject and then cut them down by half. Far better for you to set out to write 1500 words and no more. For an example of how this can be done see Outline for Articles.

See also Know What You Want To Say
Revise and Rewrite

GHOSTWRITING

(c) 1980 by Martha Monigle

(This section has been contributed by Martha Monigle, novelist (*The Doll Castle*, 1975), columnist (*Back Stage*), former associate editor (*Print*), free-lancer for national magazines, consultant at writers' conferences, playwright (two off-Broadway productions). Currently teaching adult education and ghosting on the side. Martha may be contacted by writing to P.O. Box 9181, Treasure Island, FL 33740.)

How To Be a Ghostwriter

Indignation started me on a career as a ghostwriter. Five years ago I discovered that a local person of little talent or experience was acting as a ghostwriter. I resented the mishandling of the needs of beginning writers.

At that time I was conducting Writers' Workshops for the Florida Adult Education Department in Pinellas County. These workshops had developed soon after my arrival in St. Petersburg from New York, where I had been active as a free-lancer, columnist, playwright and editor.

Now, I wondered how to go about being a ghostwriter. What is a ghostwriter? How do you contact possible clients? How do you work with them?

The answer to the first question is simple: you jump in. Provided, of course, you have some professional writing background. Though my initial reaction against incompetency had led me into ghosting, I had no idea how lucrative the field could be.

The second answer lies in the dictionary definition: "a ghostwriter is defined as a professional writer or editor who accepts a finished or partly written script and assists the author to complete the script in a marketable form."

Next, you acquire clients the same way as others who launch a new business. By advertising your services. Like a doctor with his shingle out, you wait for the first patient. Your shingle is your flyer, a printed schedule of fees and

53

services. (See sidebar at end for those figures and details.)

You distribute the flyers among your friends, relatives and neighbors. You ask the library if you can tack it on the bulletin board. You go to women's clubs or fraternal organizations and request their assistance. Few refuse.

If you're a teacher, you pass the flyers around your classes. Surprisingly enough, only three students saw me privately for help with their books.

Most of my clients are working people who have yearned to get into print, yet can't take the time to go to writing classes for help in the editing and polishing of their scripts.

Your ghostwriting clientele can increase by advertising your services in local newspapers or telephone directories. If so, be sure to check the local licensing. Magazine ads, as in the *Writer's Digest*, will bring in a variety of customers. In my case I find I have sufficient clients to keep me busy without advertising.

Give yourself a catchy label. For instance, I am "The Florida Ghostwriter" with my trademark application in Washington. Have professional stationery printed with your business address.

To preserve privacy, use a mailbox for your correspondence. For that same reason I keep an unlisted telephone number. You might wish to use your home for client conference. I prefer to rent office space by the hour. You may have to search for a kind-hearted landlord to hold down expenses. Perhaps you can locate a room in your church or community building for these odd and irregular hours. Rarely do I meet clients in my home or go to their residences.

Be as businesslike as possible to command the high fees you will ask. Ordinarily, you ask for a flat fee in advance. You may find, however, that you may have to adjust your prices and schedules to the requirements of your clients. Each customer presents a different problem which makes ghosting a constant and stimulating challenge.

Do not take on a complete ghosting of a book without a signed contract and a partial payment. Here you may require a consultation with a lawyer to draw up a contract form that you can follow.

My first client, as a result of my inexpensive flyer, came

from a recommendation of a classmate in a psychology class I was taking. (Later the teacher herself became a customer.) It seemed that my classmate's neighbor had finished a novel and had been looking for somebody to help him prepare it for the market. Since he was a young man with a daytime job, he could not attend my classes. He not only revised that book according to my suggestions but is deep in a sequel of the first one. (Use weekends for such clients.)

Gradually, you will acquire clients from a word-of-mouth system. After my novel *(The Doll Castle)* appeared in 1975, I've been invited to speak at writers' conferences and to give lectures at local junior colleges and universities. These engagements give opportunities to place flyers on conference tables and campus bulletin boards.

The most important part of your new career will be learning how to work with your clients to give them the greatest assistance.

The first contact usually comes in the mail. You agree on the fee (by letter or phone) and the estimated time for the ghosting. You evaluate the script after it arrives, write a critique and mail it off.

By trial and error I evolved the following method to prepare a critique that will be helpful to the beginning writer. I start with the heading "Overall View" for a criticism of about five or six pages, single-spaced, for books. Short stories or articles will have fewer pages. I end with a separate section, "Line-by-line Analysis," averaging three to four pages, single-spaced.

You begin the overall summary with any favorable items—characterization, atmosphere, dialog, dramatic scenes or writing style. Next, you point out the flaws without being overly critical. It is your duty as an honest ghostwriter to be able to detect errors and to offer specific suggestions for correction.

For example, since many beginners fail to establish a definite goal or purpose for fiction or nonfiction, I indicate plausible goals as gleaned from the material; I show places where goals can strengthen the script. In the novel this goal must be nearly insurmountable and not won (or lost) by the main character until obstacles and conflicts are resolved satisfactorily at the end.

55

Because the opening sets the tone of any material, I stress the importance of a good first chapter in novels, a narrative hook for stories or an intriguing lead for articles. Frequently, I rewrite the beginning in ways I feel will attract editors.

In my critiques I try to eliminate words like "plot" or "theme"as they tend to confuse the already bewildered newcomer. Instead, I recommend a "thread" to weave a pattern in the script. That thread will automatically provide a plot.

The second part of the critique, the line-by-line review, constitutes the most instructive part for the writer, but perhaps the most tedious for the ghost.

You jot down consecutive numbers on the margins of the client's script every time you spot errors. These mistakes might be minor ones in spelling, grammar or punctuation. (I am so impatient with the lavish and incorrect use of semicolons that I banish them from my students' work.) You also number the exact locations of major flaws as in unrealistic dialog, awkward transitions, boring repetitions, overlong scenes, clarification needs. These numbers are necessary so that the writer can match them on the sheets you write on the detailed analysis.

For example, I might indicate error three on page one and error 15 on page 11 in this way:

p. 1. No. 3 — identify the speaker

p. 11 No. 15 — this scene can be condensed in a paragraph without dialog.

Since my novelists prefer to deliver their scripts in person, we may have a brief conference at my "office," at which time I collect my fee in advance. If such an initial meeting lasts over half an hour, I warn them that my hourly fee will commence. That same rule for charging for my time applies on the collecting of the script and my critique. Any further conferences on their revisions patterned on my critique are placed on an hourly rate.

Once a lawyer client grumbled at the price of our conference after his revision of the opening chapters that I had to study while he waited.

"You charge as much as I do," he said.

"We are both professionals," I reminded him.

In all my critiques I try not to be too critical or discouraging because my goal is to help the author to revise and to polish the script. I also try to persuade them to do all the writing.

Another of my ghosting services is to assist writers in composing queries for articles (never for short stories) or books. I recommend these queries (written according to my techniques) as editors now demand them. Also it saves time and postage for the author. Again I charge on an hourly rate.

Here are some final tips for new ghostwriters. Never accept a script on an offer to split the sales. Never promise anything definite on the sale of a script. You promise only to give your knowledge and practical experience. You do not act as an agent though you may suggest possible markets.

You can earn more money as a fulltime ghostwriter in a year than as a free-lancer in today's tight market. Perhaps also you will find unexpected satisfaction in helping those who are stumbling on the road to becoming a published writer. My rewards in this field are not only in a financial way.

"You've told me exactly what I wanted to know about my book," said a first novelist last week at our final conference. "Now I know the path to follow."

Ghostwriter Fee Schedule Reading and Editing Fees

Articles:	Up to 1500 words	$25
	Each additional 1000 words (or fraction thereof)	5
Short Stories:	Up to 3000 words	25
	Each additional 1000 words (or fraction thereof)	5
Poetry:	Up to 30 lines	10
	Up to 75 lines	20
	Up to 100 lines (limit)	25
Plays:	One-act	50
	Two-or-Three Act Plays	125
TV or Radio:	Half hour (or less) in standard TV or radio format	75
	Hour show (or up to 90 minutes)	100
Novels:	(Adult or Juvenile) Up to 75,000 words	150
	Each additional 1000 words (or fraction thereof)	25
Nonfiction Books:	Same as novels	
Book Query:	One to three page proposal plus two ghostwritten chapters	$500
Flat Fee Books:	Complete ghostwritten book (fiction or nonfiction) with down payment of half the fee, half on completion in specified time period, usually six months	$2,500
Hourly Rate:	For research, collaboration or ghostwriting	25

GRAMMAR AND SPELLING

Misspellings and poor word usage offend the eyes of readers and editors alike, and yet they appear almost every day in newspapers and magazines, on public signs, television commercials, and advertisements of all kinds. Catchy slogans that are grammatically incorrect have helped to erode our language. They encourage us to write ungrammatically.

If you are uncertain of how to spell a word you should look it up in your dictionary. I say "your" because a dictionary is an indispensable tool for any writer and you must have one near your typewriter, stationery, and other writing supplies.

When in doubt about the accuracy of spelling, you should double check to relieve that doubt. But what if you are unaware that you have misspellings in your copy? How can you correct spelling and grammatical errors if you don't know they exist? The solution is to get someone else to read over your copy before you send it out. By doing this they should catch any errors that eluded your critical review.

A number of dictionaries are available on the market to suit any pocket or need (See list below.) Although Webster's is the preferred dictionary by many publishers, the Random House dictionary is favored by many scholars. You do not need them all.

Unabridged Dictionaries
> *The Random House Dictionary of the English Language.* Editor: Jess Stein, Random House, NY. 1966. (Abbreviations, biography, geography listed in the main part of the book. Supplementary material; atlas of the world, gazetteer of place names, dictionaries of French, German, and Italian.)
> *Webster's Third New International Dictionary of the English Language.* G & C Merriam Co., Springfield, MA. 1961 (Preliminary pages on spelling, plurals, capitalization, and punctuation.)

Abridged Dictionaries

    The American College Dictionary. Random House, NY. 1966.

    The American Heritage Dictionary of the English Language. Editor: William Morris. American Heritage Publishing Co., NY. 1969.

    The Concise Oxford Dictionary of Current English. Sixth Edition edited by J.B. Sykes. Oxford University Press, Oxford, England. 1976.

    Funk & Wagnall's Standard College Dictionary. Harcourt, Brace & World, Inc. NY. 1963.

    Webster's Seventh New Collegiate Dictionary. G & C Merriam Co. Springfield, MA. 1963.

A conventional dictionary lists words alphabetically and gives you their meanings. But what if you can't think of the word but you know the meaning? Don't despair. Turn to *Bernstein's Reverse Dictionary* for help. Published by Quadrangle: The New York Times Book Co., NY, this unconventional dictionary lists an array of meanings alphabetically and gives you their words. It helps you discover the words that you have momentarily forgotten or those you never knew, or those of whose meanings you were not quite certain.

Grammar Texts

Keep a grammar text near your dictionary. Use it frequently. You will improve your grammar and your writing by becoming familiar with the rules of usage and principles of composition. The beginning writer should have either the *Elements of Style* by William Strunk, Jr., and E. B. White, (published by The Macmillan Company, NY) or *The Golden Book on Writing* by David Lambuth and others, (published by The Viking Press).

Both books tell you how to write well-constructed sentences and string them together to form a paragraph. In a brief but direct approach they explain the use of words and punctuation, and give examples of words and expressions that are commonly misused.

Other texts that are equally helpful and go into this subject in more detail are:

Copperud, Roy H. *American Usage and Style: The Consensus*, Van Nostrand Reinhold Co., NY. 1980. (Copperud compares the judgments of current dictionaries of usage and gives the consensus as well as his own views on disputed points.)

Evans, Bergen. *A Dictionary of Contemporary American Usage.* Second Edition, Random House, NY. (Discussion of grammatical usage with examples.)

Harper Dictionary of Contemporary Usage, edited by William and Mary Morris, Harper & Row, NY. 1976. (A collaborative effort of 136 writers, editors, and public speakers chosen for their demonstrated ability to use the language carefully and effectively.)

If you feel you need more help and the personal explanation provided by an instructor, take a refresher course in grammar or a course in creative writing. Either of these should provide the individualized instruction you seek.

See also Style
Writing Tips

HOBBY WRITING

Here's how I sold six different stories all stemming from my hobby. I'm a keen amateur conchologist. That's a formal way of saying I like to collect and classify seashells. In the pursuit of this hobby I visit coastal areas for the purpose of collecting shells. Sometimes I go snorkeling for them. Months later, when I pore over my shell reference books and attempt to classify my finds I relive those carefree days at the beach all over again.

The pleasure is again recalled when I write about my hobby and share my experiences and knowledge with my readers. In the course of writing articles that inform and entertain I also increase my income.

I began by writing an informal essay for *Today's Family*. By giving the essay the title of "Shelling, A Family Fun Activity," I immediately tied it to the magazine's slant, the family and home. My lead began, "Beautiful reminders of a day at the beach can become fascinating collections for display at home."

A regional publication, the North Carolina *State* magazine, bought "A Primer for North Carolina Shell Collectors." In this informative article I emphasized the regional aspect of the story by describing the shells one can find along the North Carolina coast and comparing them to similar specimens found in the tropics. I mentioned some of my finds and included quotes from an interview with the author of a book on North Carolina shells. To maintain the regional interest, I briefly outlined the history of the North Carolina Shell Club and of its members who persuaded the State of North Carolina to adopt the Scotch Bonnet as the official state shell.

I sold a short, 500-word filler to an insurance magazine. I was amused to see they optimistically called it, "All About Shelling," for I had much more to write on the subject.

My next feature ran to 1500 words and sold to a military magazine, *The Army, Navy, and Air Force Times*. I called it "Pick Up On the Shell Game," and began my lead with an anecdote about a Navy man walking across the beach in the Pacific. Although I tied the introduction to leisure activities of military families abroad, the main thrust of my story informed the readers how to collect, clean, and use seashells as decoration. Color slides, taken by my husband, accompanied this feature and the published result was an attractive three-page spread in color. After publication I entered this feature in a writing contest sponsored by the Society for Technical Communications where it received an Achievement Award.

Still milking my hobby, I wrote a how-to piece called "How to Collect Seashells" for another regional magazine, *The New East*. This article explained what shells are, where to shell, and what equipment to use. A list of reference books to help in the classification of shells was also included. Photographs of shells that I had found in North Carolina waters accompanied this piece.

My most recent story on the subject of seashells, "Down by the Seashore," appeared in *International Travel News*. Pegging the story on the travel aspect of collecting shells, I gave the locations that I thought were the best for finding shells. Continuing with the travel theme I described the hotels, beaches, and water sports available at some of the places I had visited in the Caribbean and Bahamas.

By putting a different slant on the same basic set of facts, I was able to expand my hobby writing sales to six different markets. Once the initial research and first article were completed, it was a fairly simple job to produce more stories by changing the focus and including the new information I picked up every time I made another shell-collecting trip.

Other hobbies may be written up in a similar manner. Suppose you breed pedigree cats as a hobby. You might write an informative article that describes the cat as a species. You could begin by introducing the reader first to wild cats, and then to domestic cats, eventually emphasizing the breed you raise. What are its special characteristics? Markings? Is it long-hair or short? Information about societies and clubs for cat lovers could also be included in this article.

For your second story you might write an advice article on the care and feeding of cats, describing how you take care of

62

them, feed them and raise them. Reminiscences about your experiences with your cats could be used for a third story.

After you've written about your own hobbies and crafts your writing opportunities are far from exhausted. Ask your friends and neighbors about their leisure-time activities and you may discover you've got another series of saleable stories.

See also Idea Origination

IDEA ORIGINATION

Writing for the free-lance market is like working with a murky crystal ball. Ideas are all around you in vague shapes and forms but you need to bring them into sharp focus in order to write and to sell. The writer must be receptive to everything and then select and anticipate what will interest the reading public in the future.

The three common sources for ideas are:

* Reading
* People
* Personal experiences

Begin by reading your local newspaper. This is a wonderful source for stories about individuals who are famous or infamous, who have won an award, given a talk to a professional society or social club, who have overcome adversity, or invented a new product. Many of these people will be local residents easily accessible for your interview.

Newspapers, magazines, directories, and even the Yellow Pages of the telephone book, can help you in your search for ideas. A few hours browsing among the reference books in the public library should generate plenty of ideas. Don't forget to look over the consumer affairs booklets and federal and state government pamphlets.

I'm always clipping snippets out of the newspaper and putting them into my files. I keep folder categories such as, health, food, office topics, real estate buying and selling, tips on tax savings, women in the news and so on. When I accumulate enough of one category, I then select a central theme that will bind the story together so that I can write a round-up story. To make the story more suitable for the local or regional market, I will interview local or regional sources in person or by mail.

In searching for a story idea, you should avoid the mistake of many beginning writers who, when they come up with a good general idea, fail to narrow it down and to make it specific. Narrowing a theme makes it manageable.

64

Consider general topics such as investments, home ownership, insurance, fashions, cosmetics and beauty care, food
growing and preparation, restaurant guides, and health and
medical advice. All of these topics have universal appeal.
Think about ways in which you can narrow them down to
sell to a specific market.

Taking the topic of investments Stanley H. Allen, an
investment adviser, produced a story on "How to Make Big
Money: High Risk Investments," and sold it to *Harper's
Bazaar Magazine*. For the readers of this magazine his focus
was on the speculative ventures available for those who have
"extra" money they can afford to lose.

Another writer in the same magazine tackled cosmetics and
beauty care. He zeroed in on how to look beautiful on the
beach. He gave the reader tips on what make-up to use as well
as how to carry along cosmetics to the beach and to protect
them from the sun.

In a feature that appeared in a regional magazine the broad
area of home improvements was narrowed to how to make a
garden swing. The writer pegged the story to the Southern
locale by opening with the statement, "Once the centerpiece
of many traditional Southern gardens and the symbol of a
leisurely life-style, the arbor and swing remain a valid land-
scape feature."

People are the second source of ideas. Go wherever there
are people. Observe them, eavesdrop on them, and talk to
them. Learn about the basic drives that interest most people.
Attend classes and lectures, go to museums, historical
societies, concerts, plays, and movies. Before long you'll be a
rich repository of ideas.

Satisfying hunger and thirst is one of the basic drives. Ideas
for articles on this subject include nutrition, dieting and
weight control, wine lore, conservation, eating out, and food
preparation at home.

Some time ago I was invited to a seafood cookery demon-
stration. Most of the 50 people present sat and listened to the
demonstrator's remarks. I taped the demonstrator's comments
as she prepared the seafood. The following day I read a
newspaper story about the increased availability of North
Carolina seafood. That clipping joined the other material in

my file and with only a little more effort on my part I'll have another article to sell.

Another source for ideas are your own experiences: sports, hobbies, and games you enjoy; beliefs and philosophies you cherish; pet peeves and what you think should be done about them; your happiest moments; and your most embarrassing moments. Because you are writing about a subject with which you are familiar the story will turn out successfully. All these are potential money-makers if you write about them at the correct time, and slant the material to the magazine's needs.

Let's see what hobbies have to offer as a source of articles. You can write about how you participate in your own, or talk to others who share the same hobby. That should lead you to gathering quite a lot of information on growing plants, collecting stamps, making pottery, skydiving, or any of the pastimes that people pursue in their leisure hours. The general interest and specialty magazines are good markets for this type of feature story.

Don't neglect your job, the working environment, and your fellow workers as a potential source for ideas and stories. In my case I had spent many years working as a secretary. When I began writing professionally my familiarity with the office world enabled me to write and sell a number of stories about office management and secretarial shortcuts. When I learned that one of my editors was interested in publishing a story on temporary office work I joined a temporary service and wrote a story based on the office assignments I had been given.

Where do ideas come from? They come from all around you. Ideas may spring from people you meet, books that you read, thoughts that you have. Build up a stock of ideas by using a card file or folder system. The next step is to select the ideas that are worth pursuing. You do this by thinking about the readership for the idea. Who would be likely to read an article about this topic, and why? Will this appeal to anyone apart from the people involved? Has it mass appeal? Limited appeal? What markets will buy this type of feature?

An idea with mass appeal means you could approach any general interest magazine with a query. Limited appeal might confine you to a hobby magazine or specialty magazine that only covers the subject you have in mind. If the idea has limited appeal, is it worth your time to pursue it? What has already been written about the subject? Where will your story be different? What new dimensions can you offer the reader? Can you inform, instruct, inspire, or entertain the reader with this idea?

Keep all your ideas even those that in light of the above question might appear to have limited possibilities. Unsuccessful ideas now can become good ones later on because of a shift in the public's interest.

After you've selected an idea to write about check the market listings to find a specific market;

* Send for writer's guidelines
* Query the editor
* Tailor your work to that particular market
* Write to sell.

See also Market Listings
Query Letters and Outlines

INTERVIEWING

There are three ways to do an interview: by mail; by telephone; and in person. I prefer to conduct my interviews in person, but if that is impossible because of distance or time considerations I'll settle for a telephone or letter interview. Advance research is essential no matter which method of interviewing is used. Always prepare your questions before you call or visit your sources.

If it's direct information that you are after—let's say you are doing a round-up article on a specific subject such as how to diet, or make money—all you need to do is contact your pre-selected sources and ask them your questions. The responses you'll receive will probably meet the needs of a round-up or informational article but won't produce sufficient depth for the personal profile or the subjective story. For those stories it is essential that you interview in person because you can then pass on to your readers what you saw and thought during the interview as well as what you learned.

Mail Interview

Some interviews can be handled by mail using a well-worded questionnaire. I used this method to obtain information for some of the sections in this book when I mailed out a one-page questionnaire to a number of free-lance writers. (A stamped, self-addressed envelope was included with the questionnaire for the reply.) First, I placed my name and address at the top of the page and then gave the purpose of the questionnaire. Next, I listed five questions relating to writing habits. They were:

1. What is your specialty?
2. What part of the day do you find best for creative thought?
3. For writing?
4. When do you actually do your writing?
5. About how many hours a day do you write?

Underneath each question I left space for the response.

The last two questions solicited information that would be of help to the beginner writer.

6. Where do beginners have the most trouble in writing and selling their work?
7. How can they solve this problem?

Space was provided for any additional comments. At the bottom of the form I gave a date by which I wanted the questionnaire returned. All of the recipients of the questionnaire completed it and returned it to me by the specified date.

Telephone Interview

If you are planning to do a telephone interview you should call and give a brief introduction about the story you are preparing and tell the other person what it is you want from them. For example, you might start off with: "I am preparing a story for a specialized magazine, the ----------, on selling antiques. I've been talking to several dealers and I'd like to get your opinion on what's happening in the antique market these days. Are antiques still in great demand? What about the prices? Have they gone up, and by what percentage in the past couple of years?" After you've gotten replies to these questions you might continue with, "What's the most popular item you sell? What qualities do people look for in antiques? What should they be looking for?"

None of these type of questions requires that you visit the antique store; they can all be answered on the telephone. On the other hand, if you are doing a story on the display and sale of antiques then it is advisable to visit the store to see for yourself how the owner displayed his or her wares. You might even get some photographs of an especially good display.

Personal interview

The personal interview takes more time than a telephone call but provides greater scope for impromptu questions and answers. Furthermore, you can pick up clues from facial movement, clothes, even the environment in which you conduct the interview. All are essential if you are doing a profile piece on that individual.

Always call ahead to set up the personal interview. Give your name and the reasons why you want to interview that particular individual. Ask when it would be convenient for you to visit, or suggest a date yourself. If there is sufficient time before you do the actual interview, send along a copy of your prepared questions, so that your source may plan his or her responses and gather data and information that may help you write a better story.

Try to conduct your interviews in a quiet place, avoiding restaurants, airports, and other environments that have distracting background. I once did an interview in a power plant and the hum from all the machinery came out louder on my tape cassette than did the voice of the man I interviewed.

Conducting the Interview

Allow adequate time to do the interview. Don't take 15 minutes if you need an hour. On the other hand, you should be able to complete the interview in 1-1/2 hours. Be punctual and prompt.

If you want to get the most out of your interviews treat the other person as you would like to be treated yourself. Do not demand or insist that they respond to your questions. Just because you have been granted the opportunity to take up their time does not mean you can intrude in what they might consider sensitive areas.

Begin with a warm-up phase, a few general questions, and then get down to your prepared questions. Don't try to impress your sources or let them think you know more about the subject than you do. Remember, you are seeking their knowledge and information, not the other way around.

Encourage and direct the talk. Convince your sources that talking to you is good. Show that you are listening and responding. Do this with your posture, facial expressions, and short comments such as, "Good." "I see." "Yes." "And then. . .?"

During the interview use probing questions and reflective questions to produce the information you seek. Taking the story on antiques as an example, you might begin by asking, "How long have you been in the antiques business?" "Why does it appeal to you?" What do you believe are the causes of the increased interest in antiques?" Then proceed to a less personal angle, "Why are antiques a good investment?"

By using what, when, where, why, and how questions you get the other persons to respond in their own words, with their own reasons. Avoid asking questions that lead to a yes or no response. For example, don't ask,"Would you agree that antiques are popular today?" Instead the question should be phrased, "Why are antiques popular today?" Keep the talk going by using such devices as repeating a key word, leaving a sentence unfinished, looking puzzled, or curious.

If your sources refuse to respond to certain questions don't hammer away for a reply. Give them some time to think them over. Go on to something else but later on, try to slip in the unanswered questions. Sometimes rephrasing the question can help produce an answer.

Encourage your sources to use words and terms we can all understand. If they start to use professional jargon or phrases that you yourself do not understand, ask them to translate. "What does that mean?" "Would you explain that term for the benefit of my lay readers?"

I prefer to use a tape recorder during my personal interviews because it leaves me free to look at the other person and respond to their remarks. Furthermore, I find my sources answer the questions in greater length when they don't have to wait for me to get their words down on paper. Although, I have to spend additional time transcribing tape-recorded responses, I believe it helps to produce a better story with more accurate quotes than when I take handwritten notes. But, take your own notes using whatever method is most relaxing for you. There is no advantage in using a tape recorder if you are on edge and unable to pursue the interview to the fullest because of concern about the mechanics of recording.

As a writer you do more than observe and report your source's comments and actions. You act as a conductor of the ideas and feelings of other people. You must guard against the inclination to get caught up in other people's causes while interviewing them or to be swept away by someone's eloquent and enthusiastic arguments. However, don't take the opposite view and end up being antagonistic. During your interview your role is to be curious and interested.

Once you've got your story don't linger. Close the

71

interview on a friendly note. But be sure that you have given the other person an opportunity to add any last minute comments on the subject. I always ask, "Is there anything else you'd like to tell me on this subject?" You'd be surprised at the number of times I've been given my opening lead after asking this final question.

Let's review the key points of interviewing.

To Interview by Mail

* Prepare form letter or question
* State the purpose of your request
* Indicate completion date
* Include self-addressed stamped envelope for reply
* Mail

To Conduct a Telephone Interview

* Give your name and credentials
* Explain why you want to interview that person
* Ask your prepared questions

To Set Up a Personal Interview

* Call ahead
* Give your name and credentials
* Explain why you want to interview that person
* Suggest a date
* After interview write a letter of thanks.

See also Research and Note-taking

JUVENILE STORIES

There is only one unbreakable rule that applies to juvenile stories, said Jane Yolen in *Writing for Children*, and that is, "if you want to be a writer of juvenile books, you must be a reader of juvenile books. As a child I read folk tales, fantasy, Nancy Drew mysteries, horse stories, anything I could get my pudgy hands on. I read these stories still."

Over two thousand new children's books are published yearly, reported Yolen. What was once a fireside tale is now big business. The wide range of children's literature extends from adapted fairy and folk tales to realistic books about drugs, divorce, and death. It is important for anyone in the children's book field to know that bookstore sales are a very small part of children's book sales. Most childrens books. . . 80% is the conservative figure usually quoted. . . .are sold to schools and libraries, rather than to bookstores. A quick glance at any royalty report will confirm this, said Yolen.

"Any writer who thinks that in writing for children he has found a cushy way of making money has quite a surprise ending," said Jack McLarn, a frequent contributor to *Jack and Jill*, *Cricket* and other juvenile magazines.

With McLarn's permission here are some of the comments he made regarding the problems encountered in writing for the juvenile market. They appeared in his book, *Writing Part Time for Fun and Money*.

"Writing for kids, as opposed to writing for children, is one of the most complex undertakings a writer ever faces. Kids' tastes, their viewpoints, their vocabularies, even their thinking processes change rapidly and erratically, year to year, month to month, even age-spans too. . . .the writer who sends a six-year-old-type story to a book that courts nine-year-old readers is inviting a fast rejection."

Children, or kids as McLarn calls them, want to read about others like themselves. "The writer who would write for kids has to learn how to use the oldest writing gimmick of all. To write for kids, they must become the kid they are writing

73

about, and the kids they are writing for.''

McLarn explained further about the restrictions one has to follow when writing juvenile stories. "First, kids want the characters they read about to be kids, not watered down grown-ups.'' The lead character must be in the first scene, and the spotlight must be focused on that character all through the story.

Second, there must always be a problem, one involving the lead character. The problem must be solved or resolved, practically always by the lead. It's okay to have a grown-up help solve the problem, but the grown-up must be motivated by the kids in the story, said McClarn.

A mistake many of us make, he continued, is to begin a story with adults talking about their offspring. "Nothing turns a kid off more quickly than that device. Start with the kid, age, background characteristics; enough detail to enable the young reader to create a word picture. Let the story grow and develop through the eyes, the ears, the voice of the kid. And let it end happily. Always happily, with the reader feeling as rewarded and satisfied as the subject of the story is.''

The juvenile periodical market wasn't profitable when McLarn broke into it; "and it still isn't, he said. "The word length is still tight, the editors exacting, the requirements narrow, and the pay—well, shall we say it isn't all that generous, except for one magazine that pays up to 25 cents per word, an amazing sum for any publication. But it is a cheerful, happy, challenging field; one in which the writer will learn about human nature—small-fry type and otherwise.''

KILL FEES

If you are a nonfiction writer you should strive to get an assignment instead of writing on speculation. An assignment is a commitment by the editor that she is interested in having you write a particular story for her magazine and the story will be bought on completion. When making an assignment some magazines may even agree to pay all or part of your telephone, travel, and research expenses. Many even offer a "kill fee" arrangement along with the assignment.

A kill fee is more pleasant than it sounds. It is the fee paid to you by a magazine in the event the decision is made not to use the story that you were originally commissioned or assigned to write. You can be sure that if an editor wants your story badly enough to offer a kill fee that editor will work closely with you to produce a completely usable article. You may be asked to make minor changes or rewrite part because it is unlikely that the assigned story would be rejected by the magazine. The only circumstance when rejection might occur is when there has been a change of editorial policy or editorship between the time you were given the assignment and the time you completed it.

The kill fee is usually agreed upon before you begin writing. It may be as much as half or as little as one-third to one-fifth of the usual payment for a completed story. To avoid any misunderstandings the terms of the kill fee should always be worked out in advance. If the editor doesn't refer to it in her assignment letter it is quite acceptable for you to raise this point. Letting the editor know that you are aware of such details only enhances your professional image.

The kill fee is only a fee to recompense you for your time. It does not give the magazine the right to permanently kill your story. The story must be returned to you if it is rejected. In the event that a magazine decides not to use your feature and pays you a kill fee, the story then becomes your property once again and you are free to sell it elsewhere.

See also Editors' Responses

KNOW WHAT YOU WANT TO SAY

"Before you can hope to write clearly you must first think clearly," said Robert Clawson, a communications specialist. Clawson was instructing a group of government scientists on how to write technical papers when he made that remark, but it applies equally to all kinds of writing. Whether you are writing fiction or features you must devote ample time to think through what you want to write before you can set words down on paper.

Think First—Write Second

Carry a small notebook with you at all times. Never be without it. When your thinking really gets into gear about your project you are prone to get some of your best ideas at the strangest time and in the strangest places. Be prepared to make some jottings just before you go to bed, or over morning coffee, when you come out of the shower, waiting in your car at a stop light, grocery shopping,. . .any time. Ideas have come to me at all these times, but I find ironing clothes seems to trigger my writing thoughts best.

Ruth Moose finds the early morning best for her creative thought. "But my best ideas come any times; while driving, just before bed, brushing my teeth. Or as Catherine Drinker Bowen said, 'Writing is not apart from living. Writing is a kind of double-living.' "

Dennis Hensley does his thinking very early in the morning or late at night. Bette Elliott is another writer who finds the best time for creative thought is very early in the morning. Martha Monigle's best creative time is early morning, while taking her sunrise walk on the beach. Jack McLarn does his creative thinking, "usually in the afternoons, to keep from cutting the grass," he said.

If you can find a willing listener, discuss your thoughts with him. The discussion should help to fix your ideas clearly in your own mind before you attempt to put them in writing.

Never start a piece of writing of any kind without knowing the answers to the following questions: 1. Why am I writing? (Purpose) 2. For whom am I writing? (Audience) and 3. What reaction do I want? (Result).

Keep distilling your answers to these questions until you can put the answer for each into a single sentence. You might go over the checklist provided by Carl Goeller in his book, *Writing to Communicate.* He suggests that you decide:

What do I want to say?
Who will be my audience?
Why will this interest them?
How much do they already know about this topic?
What can I tell them that they don't know?
What can they do with this information?
Do I have the research to cover the topic adequately?
If I leave the reader with only one point, what do I want it to be?
What is my conclusion and what do I recommend?

If your answer to any of the above is negative, Goeller advises you take another look at your proposed writing project. Perhaps you need more facts. Have you all your research at hand before you start writing? "Be prepared to write a longer article than you need, then edit it." Goeller believes editing is much easier than back-tracking to dig up more material.

How many points should you cover? This varies according to the space allotted to the topic. Three points are a good, workable number and ten are maximum, according to Goeller. If you have more than ten points to make in your article, consider writing a series of two or more articles or even a book.

When you begin to arrange your main ideas into some order you may have difficulty in deciding which main idea you want to put first, which second, and so on. "This is an individual problem with each writer," said Clawson. "The important thing is to decide upon the approach you wish to take. Then arrange your ideas in the order that will lead your reader, step by step, systematically and logically to your

77

conclusion. Once you have arranged your main ideas in an order, you will notice that they have fallen into a definite pattern or sequence.

Don't Rely On Your Memory

A mental outline develops in your mind when you have been thinking about a story or article for a long period of time and have reached the point where you know what you want to say. Don't be tricked into commencing to write without first preparing a written outline. Without the aid of a prepared outline, words and phrases that add up to a step-by-step procedure, there's a good chance you may wander and lose track of your original intentions.

See also Formula for Features
Outline for Articles

LEADS

Writers do a lot of fishing. We must fish for and hook editors with query letters, and later we put out more bait in the form of a "lead" to pique the interest of our readers. The types of leads are limited only by your own imagination. You might choose to open your story with a question to arouse curiosity or an intriguing fact or a controversial statement that will goad the reader into a "prove-it-to-me" reaction. The case history or anecdotal lead is a good beginning for many nonfiction articles.

It is also quite acceptable to compose a lead that is based on the reporter's system of five W's and H—who, what, when, where, why, and how. In fact, the answer to any of these questions may produce the most important point you wish to make in your story.

Some of the leads I have used and sold are:

A *teaser* lead, a statement made to attract the reader's curiosity opened my story, "Reston, Virginia, Life in A Goldfish Bowl," that appeared in the *North Carolina Architect Journal.* I wrote:

> When I arrived in Reston in 1968 the population was under 5,000. Five years later it had quadrupled to over 20,000. Those five years spent in Reston were, as one resident put it, "Like living in future shock every day." (The story told what happened in that town.)

A *statement of fact* lead opened an informative nonfiction article, "Don't Poison Your Pet," for *Today's Family.*

> Thousands of pets are poisoned every year in the United States and the number is increasing. Although malicious poisoning does occur, most cases of animal poisoning are accidental, due to

human carelessness. However, an alert and informed pet owner can help prevent the death or illness of her pet. (The article told how.)

A long *picture* lead, describing the Jamaican setting in which the story took place, was used for "The A3 Does Not Go to Portsmouth," published by *Town and Country Planning Journal.*

> The coast road from the airport is a narrow lane overlooked by small and large estates. Plantations, old great houses, and tiny country towns dot the hillside. Snaking by resort hotels and sugar-cane fields, some of which are now being developed into housing estates, the life of the country appeared before us as we turned each bend on the main north-coast road. Occasionally a glimpse of the rocky, rugged coastline or sandy bays would flash into view. With much hornhonking, trucks loaded with sugar-cane swerved past on the curves and bends that may be more appealing to a race-track driver than to the tourist trying to get from one part of the island to another.

Note the difference in style between this lead and the one I used for the pet article.

A taut lead, less than 50 words long, told readers what they would learn from my how-to-do-it travel feature, "Chartering a Yacht in the British Virgin Islands," that appeared in *International Travel News.* It began:

> Chartering a yacht has much to offer. A sailing vacation that takes you away from speed, pressure, and hassle. Being on the sea is different from being by the sea, said my husband on his return from a charter in the British Virgin Islands.

At this point the reader would be hooked wanting to know why on the sea was different from by the sea.

Anecdotal leads are popular for features. I wrote this one

80

for *Woman's Life*. My feature called "The New Woman," was about women in non-traditional jobs.

> "We recently hired a woman as a telephone lineman," reported Mr. Gary M. McKelvey, Operations Manager of the Chapel Hill Telephone Company. "This is an outdoor job and involves working with a four or five man crew. A lot of work is done from ladders and buckets and I would expect that she's going to be up in the air by some means or other. I don't know how often she'll have to climb a telephone pole, but I've an idea that she's going to want to learn how to do it, even if she doesn't need to," he surmised enthusiastically.

Secretarial students and their instructors were enticed by a leading *question* to read my story about typewriter keyboards. "Will ASK replace QWERTY?" ran in *Office Skills* in Great Britain. It began:

> How would you like to type 150 words per minute? Free of errors? It can be done. Mrs. Barbara Blackburn, an American secretary, has a cruising speed of 150 to 160 w.p.m. and says she has gone as high as 170 w.p.m. Blackburn's skill earned her the label, "The World's Fastest Typing Secretary."

How Long a Lead Should You Write?

Newspaper reporters are told to keep the lead short, but feature article and fiction writers are free of this restriction. The exact length of a lead varies depending upon the type of material you are writing, the length of the piece, and the publication in which it will appear. Sometimes it takes two or three paragraphs to present a lead. That is perfectly acceptable for stories that run to 1500 words or more. However, if space restrictions require that you complete the story in 700 words or less you'll have to jump right in with a short snappy lead.

Regardless of the type or length of lead you use, once you've captured your readers don't let them go. Retain their interest by using smooth transitions, and an ongoing pace that will make your story end as powerfully as it began.

See also Revise and Rewrite
Writing Tips

LEGAL INFORMATION FOR THE WRITER

In order to recognize and avoid legal problems arising from something you've written you must be familiar with the laws that govern published writing. A writer may be held responsible for violation of the laws of libel, invasion of privacy, and fair use. The following information is given only as a guide to explain fundamental principles. Consult your lawyer if you need further guidance or have any doubts about the propriety of releasing a story or interview for publication.

The First Amendment

The rights of freedom of speech and of the press are protected under the First Amendment to the Constitution of the United States. The First Amendment says that the Federal Government cannot keep us from saying, writing, or printing anything we wish. In practice, we are free to enjoy these rights only so long as we do not hurt someone else.

The First Amendment does not make a distinction between free-lance writers, and staff writers or professional journalists. "They are equally protected or equally vulnerable, depending on one's point of view," wrote William E. Francoise in *Law and The Writer.*

Under the First Amendment a writer has more protection and less restriction when writing about public officials and public figures than when delving into the lives of private citizens. For example, truth is a complete defense if proven in a libel suit, but whether it is in good taste, or fair, or ethical, is another matter entirely. Lawsuits may succeed if the individual can show "actual malice" on the part of the publisher or writer, even if a story is "true."

Familiarize yourself with the libel law and the law of privacy if you are going to write about real people. You're fairly safe as long as you are stating an opinion that deals with a matter of public interest. If you review a book, movie, play, or restaurant you are protected by the right to fair comment or opinion, no matter how scathing your comments.

83

The demands of accuracy and objectivity in news-reporting should be balanced with the demands of fair play. We frequently hear that the public has a right to be informed. However, the public's right to know should be balanced with the question of good taste. We are no longer in the era of sensational journalism. In printing the news, morbid or sensational details of criminal behavior should not be exploited.

Libel

Libel laws vary from state to state, but the general agreement is that injury must not be done to an individual's reputation. If you attack an individual's reputation in print you may get slapped with a lawsuit. The lawsuit, however, may be dismissed if the plaintiff cannot prove identification and a harmful effect.

Watch out for your description of a living person even if you camouflage that person by giving him a fictitious name. If the description, physically or otherwise, identifies the individual to those in his immediate area the story has effectively named him. Should the story be detrimental to that person's reputation, social acceptance, business, or profession, you may lose the suit. Don't take unnecessary risks.

The Right of Privacy

When a person becomes involved in a news event, voluntarily or involuntarily, he or she forfeits the right to privacy. Similarly, a person involved in a matter of legitimate public interest normally can be written about with impunity. However, news writers and editors are cautioned by *The Associated Press Stylebook and Manual* that this does not permit the publication of a story that dredges up damaging details of an individual's past that have no relevance to current newsworthiness.

Before submitting a story for publication scrutinize it for accuracy and fairness using this guide:

Is the article newsworthy?
In the public interest?
Is it accurate and objective?

Is it free of malice?

Is it in good taste?

Free from exploitation of morbid or sensational details of criminal behavior?

Are you invading the privacy of the individual?

Is the person's reputation injured?

Does it disclose any private facts which might be offensive or embarrassing?

Copyright Law

> "When you take stuff from one writer, it's plagiarism; but when you take it from many writers, it's research." Wilson Mizner

The rights of an author in an unpublished manuscript are protected by common law. After publication, unless the published work carries a legal notice of copyright, it may become public property, falling into "the public domain." (See Copyright Law and Registration Procedures.)

How can you avoid infringing on the copyright of others? The question of fair use is often brought up at writers' conferences. Some helpful guidelines are provided by Marjorie E. Skillin, in *Words Into Type.* "Quotation is not always infringement," she wrote. "Long custom has recognized the right of reviewers to quote passages of sufficient length to illustrate their criticism and indicate the quality of the book under review." This degree of quotation is permitted under the concept of "fair use."

Quotations that are complete units in themselves, as in the case of poems, letters, short stories, maps, charts, tables, or other illustrative materials, are never considered fair use. Skillin explains that, "in interpreting the law, the courts look to the nature, quantity and value of the material used and determine whether its use was unfair to the quoted author." The number of words quoted plays less importance than the question of whether the quotation injures the worth of the original. Does the new work compete for the same market? The simplest way to avoid infringement is to protect yourself by securing written permission from the copyright owner before you turn in your final copy to the publisher.

There is no copyright on ideas or information, only on the form in which they are expressed. Writers should be mindful of the possibility of subconscious plagiarism, says John B. Adams, professor of journalism at the University of North Carolina in Chapel Hill. "It stretches the imagination to believe that every person who writes is totally creative and creates something brand-new. Everybody who does any writing should be aware that in their minds are scores of words strung together in a given sequence. And, when they are writing a piece or a book they come forth," Adams told me.

"There's no way most people can remember where those words came from. If something flows from your mind as if it were the result of pushing a number of buttons, then rewrite it. Because you might have regurgitated something you've already read. If it comes too easily, be suspicious," says Adams, noting that, "you have to work on words. They come one at a time for most people."

As for fiction, here the writer is presumably creating every word and the series of words or sequence in which they appear. "But even so, when writing fiction you should be careful about using real persons as model for your characters. Use imaginary people with imaginary names, and have them affected by imaginary incidents," says Adams.

Language of the Law

Writers of mystery and detective stories and nonfiction writers, should be familiar with the language of the law, as well as points of law, criminal actions, and courtroom procedures so that they may present to their readers an accurate picture of the law. To write credibly about legal practices and criminal procedures you need to understand these activities yourself.

"Because procedures and practices vary from state to state you should get a copy of current law and criminal procedures in your state, or the state in which your story action takes place," advises Adams.

In addition, contact your local district attorney or prosecuting attorney for an explanation of basic court procedures. Other sources of information for the writer are legal libraries, court officials, and state and local bar associations, whose members are both prosecuting and defense attorneys. Information on legal aid and other social services provided to citizens may be found by calling these agencies in your area.

The American Bar Association has prepared a layman's handbook of court procedures, with a glossary of legal terminology. To obtain the handbook, *Law and the Courts*, send fifty cents to the American Bar Association, 1155 East 60th Street, Chicago, IL 60637.

For further information on libel and other laws read:

Angione, Howard, *The Associated Press Stylebook and Libel Manual*, The AP Press, New York.

Ashley, Paul P. *Say It Safely*. Univ. of Washington Press, Seattle, WA.

Glassman, Don. *Writers' & Artists' Rights*, Writers Press, Washington, DC.

Polking, Kirk. and Leonard S. Meranus, editors, *Law and The Writer*, Writer's Digest Books, Cincinnati, OH

*See also Copyright Law and Registration Procedures
Photograph Releases*

MANUSCRIPT PREPARATION AND MAILING

Paper

For rough drafts I use yellow second sheets. They are cheaper than white bond paper and the color helps to distinguish drafts from final copies. I type the final copy of a manuscript on letter-size (8-1/2 x 11 inches) white bond of good quality. I prefer to use a 20 lb bond of 25% cotton fiber, although the 16 lb weight is acceptable to editors. I don't like special erasable papers because although they do their job of making it easy for the typist to erase they have a tendency to smear when touched.

Equipment

Many professionals prefer to use the pica, or large, type for their manuscripts. They say the elite, or small type, is hard on an editor's eye. However, I've been using my IBM Selectric$^{(R)}$ with elite type for many years without hearing any complaints. The Selectric$^{(R)}$ is a versatile machine because it has a small globe-shaped printing element containing type characters instead of typebars. Type styles can be changed by snapping off one element and snapping on another. A number of different style elements are available. Whatever type style is used, the purpose is to produce a manuscript with a neat, clear appearance, very easy to read. Try to avoid script, italics, Old English, or other unusual type characters. These are not welcomed by editors.

If your typewriter has typebars instead of an element, be sure they are clean before you commence typing your manuscript. In particular check the letters a, b, c, d, e, g, o, p, q, s, and u to make sure they are not filled-in with ink from the ribbon. Carbon ribbons are less likely to cause this problem than inked-fabric ribbons.

Layout

Your name and address should be typed single space in the left hand corner. Center the title in capital letters. Two spaces

88

below the title write "By" and your name or pen name on the same line. (See example below.) If you are using a pen name, it should appear in the "by-line" and your real name should be given with the address in the left hand corner. No explanation is necessary regarding the difference between the two names.

Indicate the rounded word-count on the top right hand corner. Estimate the number of words by multiplying the average words in a line by the number of lines on a full page by number of pages, i.e., 10 words a line times 25 lines times 6 pages equals 1500 words.

Your name   Copyright (c) Your Name 198—
Street Address   Rights Offered
Town, State, Zip Code   Approximate Number of Words

Social Security No.

Submitted to _____ Magazine

TITLE IN CAPITALS

by Your Name

Commence text by indenting paragraph 5 spaces. Begin two double spaced lines below your name.

Copyright notice is included to indicate that this is your own original work and you wish to protect the manuscript. The title is placed about three inches from the top of the page, or two double spaced lines after the name of the magazine. Text begins two double-spaced lines below your name.

Margins and Spacing
By leaving a 1-1/2 inch margin on the left side, and one inch at top, bottom and right side, you are left with a 6-inch

typing line that averages ten words. Double space all copy. Indent paragraphs five spaces only. Do not begin a paragraph on the last line at the bottom of a page, unless the paragraph is of only two lines and can be finished on that page. Preferably carry the two lines over as a good beginning for the new page.

Type on one side of the paper only. On succeeding pages, type your last name and/or an identifying title word before each page number, viz. "Berman — A-Z Writing 2." Indicate the end of your manuscript by using either the sign-off signal "30," or by writing "End."

Even if someone else types your manuscript it is still your responsibility as author to proofread the copy. Proofreading is a job that has to be done practically word by word, sentence by sentence, rather than in terms of the clarity of the ideas or the efficiency of the sentence. Try to get someone to proofread with you. Errors are easier to detect if the copy is read aloud than if you attempt to check the material yourself by comparing line by line. Let the other person check your final typed copy while you read aloud from the rough draft.

Always make a carbon copy, or photocopy, of your story for your files so that you have a record of it in case it gets lost in the mail, or on some editor's desk. When making the rounds with your manuscripts be sure they look fresh, not dog-eared, even if they have been rejected by other markets. Sometimes this means retyping all or part of the manuscript, but it's worth it. A clean manuscript indicates professionalism, and the editor will never know it has been rejected. With my method of putting the magazine's name on the first page of my manuscripts I always have to retype that page, usually all that is needed to produce a fresh appearance.

Mailing Manuscript

If your manuscript is your first approach to an editor a cover letter is unnecessary. Let the manuscript speak for itself. If you are submitting a manuscript as a result of a query and a confirming "go-ahead" from the editor, then write a cover letter with this explanation so that your manuscript doesn't end up in the "unsolicited" pile.

Always enclose a stamped, self-addressed return envelope

otherwise the editor will not feel obliged to return your work. Do not send cash or a check for the return postage.

Send all manuscripts flat no matter how few the number of pages. A flat page is more convenient to read than a page that has been creased in folds, so a flat manuscript has a better psychological effect on the reader. Never send a manuscript rolled. Do not staple pages. Use a paper clip only to keep pages together. Some writers place a small piece of paper, or an envelope corner, on top of the pages before they put on the paper clip.

Packaging

If you use a 9-1/2 x 12-1/2 inch envelope for the outer envelope it will take your manuscript and a 9 x 12 inch return envelope. I happen to use the 9 x 12 inch size for both the outer and return envelopes and merely fold the return envelope in half so that it "hugs" the manuscript.

Send large manuscripts, such as books, in a cardboard box or between cardboards bound with rubber bands. Write your name and address on the cardboard as well as the name and address of the person or company to whom it is being sent. Wrap it in heavy brown paper.

Mailing

I mail all my manuscripts First Class. Manuscripts that weigh more than 12 ounces may be sent by First Class "Priority" mail. The postage rate varies according to the zone.

To save money you can send packages via Fourth Class marked "Special Handling." In addition to the required postage, there is a fee for adding the words "Special Handling." Manuscripts and books that are sent at the Special Fourth Class rate may have a personal letter enclosed but you must also add sufficient First Class postage to cover the letter, and mark on the outside of your package, "First Class Letter Enclosed."

Check with your local post office for further details and current rates of postage. Insufficient postage might mean the return of your package by the Post Office or unacceptance by the person to whom it is addressed.

See also Typing Tips

MARKET LISTINGS

How to Understand Market Listings

To get the most out of market listings read them carefully and always follow the editor's directions. Send for a sample copy of the magazine and writers' guidelines if they are offered. If a listing indicates that only queries are invited, don't send a completed manuscript. Send a letter or outline about your proposed feature and ask if the editor is interested. (See Query Letters and Outlines.)

Queries are unnecessary for fiction or poetry submissions because the editor will want to read the completed piece before making any commitment to buy.

What kinds of information can you expect to find in a market listing? At the very least you will learn the name and address of the publication, the audience it serves, the kinds of material published, the acceptable length of manuscripts, the method of payment, and the rights purchased. Some listings are more detailed. They tell you the year the publication was established, the circulation figures, and whether they will read completed manuscripts or if you should query first. Listings may also mention the style of writing preferred, the average time it takes for the editor to report back to you, the availability of free sample copies, or the cost of such copies. Some markets will even tell you the amount they pay as a kill fee.

Just for your practice in reading a market listing I've prepared a fictitious example. Let's say it is:

> The Castleber Magazine, 113 Memory Lane, Anyplace, 99999. Monthly. Rita Berman, Editor. 80-96 pages. 70% free-lance written. Established 1972. Circ. 25,000.
>
> Our audience is primarily affluent, early retirees, hard-working above-average executives, and tourist-oriented folks.
>
> Sample copy $1.50; free writer's guidelines for SASE. Submit seasonal/holiday material 3-4 months

in advance of issue date. Reports in 2-3 weeks. Buys all rights but may reassign following publication. Pays on acceptance. By-line given.

Nonfiction: Castleber magazine is a broad-based magazine interested in receiving short, factual, how-to articles concerned with food, money, sports, or travel topics. Maximum length 1000 words. Also buys first-person stories of life in other countries. Some interviews by assignment; some nostalgia; must be well-written, not maudlin. Photo feature: profile, and travel. Buys 30-40 mss/year. Query or submit complete manuscript. Length 500-1500 words. When appropriate, articles should be accompanied by good 35 mm color transparencies or sharp, contrasty b/w glossy prints. Pays approximately 15 cents/word but varies depending on the name of the author, quality of work, importance of article. Pays $7.50 for each b/w photo. Pays $15.00 each for color photo. Kill fee 35% on assignment.

Fiction: Rebecca Brown, fiction editor. May include, but is not limited to, adventure, historical, fantasy, mystery, and romance. All stories need plot structure, action and incident. Humor is highly desirable. Buys 10 mss/year. Length 500-1500 words. Pays approximately 5 cent/word.

Poetry: Free verse and traditional. Buys 2-3/issue. Length 1 page maximum. Pays $10.

Fillers: Short items similar to nonfiction above. Payment varies $5-7.50/filler.

How to break in: New authors should obtain current issues of the magazine and study them to find out our present needs. We would reject a story by the world's best known author if it didn't fit our needs.

What does this fictional composite tell you? To begin with

you learn the periodical is a monthly publication and is 70% free-lance written. That clearly indicates they need you. They have a mature, monied audience, so you wouldn't want to send in stories aimed at stay-at-home teenagers.

Sample copies are not free but the writers' guidelines are. They put out a holiday number and report fairly promptly. They may reassign rights following publication but the choice is the publishing company's, not yours. They pay on acceptance so you get your money ahead of publication. Your disappointment will be lessened if the story is not run later because you will already have received your money.

You get a by-line which is helpful in building up clips of published work. This listing is a wide-open field for nonfiction. Almost anything will sell here, as long as it is well-written. You may query or submit a complete manuscript. If you want to do an interview, however, you must query ahead to get the assignment. A kill fee is paid on assignments so it is worth taking the time to query.

It is not a good market for fiction, despite the range published, because it only uses ten stories a year. In order to break in they suggest you send in material similar to that already been published.

I created the preceding listing in order to avoid singling out any one particular market for analysis. However, there are thousands of genuine listings available in *The Writers' and Artists' Year Book, The Writer's Handbook* and the *Writer's Market.* See also Walter G. Oleksy's *1,000 Tested Money-making Markets for Writers,* published by Barnes and Noble.

No matter which source you use to locate listings always read them thoroughly and entirely. Submit your work to the right market. If a listing tells you the editor wants hunting and fishing stories, don't send a feature on disco dancing. Send stories on catching fresh and saltwater fish, or on water safety rules. Make sure you spell the name of the editor correctly. Do send along a couple of clippings of your published work if they are similar to your proposed feature.

Don't limit your market research to a single category. An article about collecting seashells, for example, could be sold to a craft or hobby magazine, a regional magazine, and a

94

general interest, or women's interest magazine.

Finally, always include a self-addressed stamped envelope when you query an editor or send in a completed manuscript. Most magazines will not respond without an SASE, and you may not get your manuscript returned. The market listings are your most efficient way to find a broad market for your work. Studied well and used wisely, the listings can save you an immense amount of time.

See also Query Letters and Outlines
Selling Your Writing

MULTIPLE SALES OF ARTICLES

(c) 1980 By Dennis E. Hensley

(This section has been contributed by Dennis E. Hensley a free-lance writer in Indiana who has published more than 1,000 articles in a variety of magazines and newspapers, including such trade publications as *The Writer* and *Writer's Digest*. He is a frequent instructor at writers' conferences, and he is a director of the Manchester College Writers' Workshop.)

A few years ago I learned that I could train my ears and eyes to detect article ideas everywhere I went. What's more, by applying a few professional modifications, I found I could resell one original news item to several statewide newspapers and national magazines. You can do the same thing by following a few basic steps.

When selling one article idea to multiple markets, I use a marketing approach geared to ever-enlarging circles. I sell first to the city paper ($8-15), then to the large statewide papers ($50-$60 for magazine supplements), then to the regional periodicals ($50-$75), then to the national outlets ($75 and up), and whenever possible, to international publications ($50 and up).

Each time I resell the article idea, I try to make the new version different in at least three ways: (1) I provide photos of the person or event which have not appeared in other publications; (2) I insert one or two new facts about the incident which were not emphasized in a previous article; and (3) I attempt to write the article as stylistically close to the established format of the receiving publication as possible, while also trying to gear the event to its geographical locale.

For example, an area man named Pete Schlatter invented a workable two-wheel automobile recently and I played that story for all it was worth. My first article appeared in the *Muncie Star*, with a local-boy-makes-good angle. It mentioned area people who had influenced Schlatter and gave a short history of his years in town. My next article appeared in *The*

Muncie Weekly News, a county-wide paper, with an area-resident-is-inventor angle. I next sold the article to the magazine sections of *The Indianapolis Star* and *The South Bend Tribune*, two statewide papers, with a Hoosier-man-is-unique-mechanic angle. The article covered statewide auto shows at which the car had been displayed. Afterward, I submitted the article to *Hot Rod* for national publication, focusing strictly on the auto itself, and it eventually went international when I sold it to the *Christian Science Monitor* for its overseas and Canadian editions. Milking an article is a trick of the trade for a small town writer who enjoys a worldwide audience.

I have lectured at dozens of colleges, universities, writers' clubs, workshops and conferences, and the chief flaw I have found in most beginning free-lance writers is their inability to resell their features and articles and interviews. Most novice writers labor under the idea that the job of the free-lancer is to research a topic, write a manuscript about that research, sell the manuscript to whoever will buy it, and then move on to the next assignment. If that were *really* the case, I'd be driving a truck or managing a grocery store or doing something that was a far cry from being a free-lance writer.

I would much rather sell one article six times than write six articles which will sell one time each. Robert Louis Stevenson once said, "I hate to write, but I love to have written." I'm like that, too. I enjoy playing with my kids, reading books, having dinner with friends and traveling around the country more than I like staring at a blank piece of paper, knowing that I have to create something on it that will be so captivating people will actually pay me cash for the opportunity to print it.

Writing quality articles is hard work. You have to conduct interviews, dig out research, check sources, work through several drafts of writing and then cajole editors into buying your material. It's a hassle. Like Stevenson said, when it's all over and you've got the check in hand and you see your by-line in print, you're happy; getting to that point, however, is real work.

A lot of the drudgery of free-lance writing can be eliminated when the writer sells his article a second and third time.

Checks and by-lines are still the end products, but the research and interviewing and most of the original draft writing are no longer necessary. You simply retain all rights to your articles by putting the natural copyright symbol on your manuscripts (example: (c) 1980 by Dennis E. Hensley) and then assuming ownership after each subsequent publication of your article.

My rule-of-thumb is that I never write an article unless I am confident that I can sell it (or a modified version of it) to at least four or more publications. Even seemingly minor news ideas can be sold to a variety of markets if you get the right news peg.

I was once talking to a local man I knew. He mentioned that his 65-year-old brother, Walter O. Miles, a former resident of our town, ran a printing shop in California and that for extra money he did walk-ons and bit parts in TV shows and movies. He was coming home to visit his brother; so, I set up an interview appointment.

Admittedly, Walt Miles turned out to be small pickings in the Hollywood scene, but he had been connected in minor ways to several smash movies, including a three-minute scene in "MacArthur" and a non-speaking role in "Close Encounters of the Third Kind."

I could have wasted my time writing articles like, "Another Extra Tells His Story," but there would have been nothing eye-catching about such features and they would not have sold. However, I bypassed the obvious story—the tie to Hollywood—and instead focused upon the fact that when most men were getting ready to retire, Walt Miles was beginning a new and quite glamorous career.

That news peg worked very well. I sold "He Didn't Retire: He Became a Star'" to *New England Senior Citizen;* I sold "Close Encounters of the Late in Life Kind" to *The Indianapolis Star Magazine;* I sold "Late Blooming Hoosier Actor Faces Busy Season" to *Michiana;* I sold "Actor Walt Miles Won't Retire" to the *Muncie Star;* I sold "Senior Citizen Has Unique Pastime" to *Grit;* and I sold "No Rocking Chair for Actor Walt Miles" to the *Camden Chronicle.*

I spent one afternoon visiting with Walt Miles and interviewing him. The results were six feature article sales.

Basically, I was telling the same story over and over, but each time I was telling it to new readers and I was telling it in a slightly different way. I made more than $700 from these multiple sales and saved myself a lot of time, too.

Let's follow the step by step reselling techniques I used recently when marketing an interview I conducted with Walter and Charlotte Baldwin, the mother-and-father-in-law of the Rev. Jim Jones of Guyana. In retracing my steps, we'll see how the multiple marketing process works.

When I visited the Baldwins in their home, I came prepared with dozens of questions. I tape recorded a long interview which touched on a number of topics, including their daughter's marriage and life with Jim Jones. I also asked the Baldwins to provide me with photos of their daughter, Marceline, and Jim Jones taken at their wedding and at family reunions. Additionally, I made photographs of the local school and church that Marceline and Jim had attended.

After interviewing the Baldwins, I processed my photos and wrote my feature based on the interview. I kept the first draft short, about 1,000 words. I took the draft to the editor of my local paper, the North Manchester *News Journal,* and asked if he would like to buy it. He said yes, but that his budget for free-lance material was limited. I let him print the article and two photos in exchange for $15, a by-line and two dozen free copies of the edition it appeared in. It was agreed that all ownership of the article would be mine.

Once that local article appeared in print, I sent a copy of it to the editor of the weekend magazine supplement to *The South Bend Tribune.* I asked if I could expand the article to 2,000 words and add some extra pictures and sell it to him. His paper covered most of northern Indiana and southern Michigan. He realized that very few of his readers would have seen the version I did for the North Manchester paper. He offered me $100, a by-line and four free copies of the printed version. I agreed, but again retained my ownership.

After the article broke in South Bend, I had sent a copy of it to the editor of the *Cincinnati Enquirer* (both a typed manuscript copy and a photostat of the inprint version). He knew that none of his readers would have seen the Indiana newspapers; so, he paid me $200, a by-line and five free printed copies for the rights to reprint *The South Bend Tribune* article exactly as I had written it.

I continued this same process of sending my article to different editors of different papers in different states. I never hid the fact that the article had already appeared in other newspapers. The editors never seemed to mind, so long as the other newspapers did not cross over into their circulation or readership territories.

While my general feature on the Baldwins was making its round of editors in Indiana, then Ohio, then Kentucky, then Michigan, and so on, and was earning royalty checks on a steady basis for me, I went on to a new project. I replayed my interview tapes and pulled out information I had not already covered. I produced a second manuscript, one strictly focusing upon Mrs. Baldwin's relationship with her daughter after Marceline's marriage to Rev. Jones. I then began it on the same circuit of editors.

Let's review the basic points related to multiple article sales:

First, remember to do a long interview or a lot of other research so that you'll have plenty of topics to write about.

Second, maintain copyright ownership of your articles and manuscripts.

Third, sell to the smallest markets first and then to larger and larger circulation publications.

Fourth, never get involved in researching an article that will not have enough broad appeal to sell to several different periodicals.

Resales can increase a free-lance writer's annual income by more than 60% in one year's time when used effectively. And since the whole reason for writing is to be paid for your work, why not be paid top dollar!

MY METHOD FOR SUCCESSFUL SALES

Assuming that you've already queried the editor and you know what he or she needs, how do you end up with a successful sale? In this section I will present as an example the case history of the successful sale of a business feature. I will describe the five-step method I use to research, get leads, get the interview, conduct it, and finally, put the piece together. This outline may be used as a guide for selling other nonfiction articles.

Step No. 1. Know Your Topic

You can write from personal experience, as I did about office procedures when I first began selling my writing, but to increase your sales potential you should investigate and write about the methods and opinions of others. Here's where research is absolutely essential. Step one is read and research.

Your reading should provide sufficient background knowledge about the topic so that you can ask the right qeustions and elicit the right responses from those you are interviewing. Become familiar with current business terms in order to understand what your sources are telling you. Add to your general knowledge of the subject by talking to experts in that particular field, even if you don't intend to feature them in your story.

* Read
* Investigate
* Listen and Learn.

Step No. 2. Decide Who Should be Interviewed

Although business and trade journal editors are helpful about telling you what they are looking for, they won't give you leads, and they won't tell you whom to interview. That's your job.

The easiest way to break in is to contact the larger companies in your area. Anyone who has a product to sell is a potential story. Start off with a field in which you are personally interested or one that may have interviewees read-ily accessible to you. Personnel directors, sales managers, and financial consultants are a few types that spring to my mind. These people are often quite willing to talk to writers and reporters, particularly if the story will reflect well on their company. You have something to offer them, too—free pub-licity.

So here you are—you've got some knowledge of the topic you want to handle and you have a particular person in mind to interview. The next step is where many writers get hung-up, and it may turn out to be the most difficult part of the whole project—the interview.

Step No. 3. Getting the Interview

If you don't set up that all-important interview you can't proceed with your story. I use both telephone and letter approaches to set up interviews. The telephone approach is normally the simplest, most direct way to get an interview. If I have read about an individual and decided that he might supply the information I need, or have been referred to him by someone else, I call and ask for an appointment. In the ensuing conversation I explain why it is I want to do an interview. Over the telephone your sources are able to discuss any reservations they may have about granting an interview. Overcome their objections by reassuring them that you don't do "hatchet jobs," and assure them that your business stories are positive, upbeat, how-to-succeed stories.

Writing in this field requires patience, hard work, thorough-ness, and persistence. You can't take "no" for an answer if your whole story depends on obtaining an interview from one particular person. You will have to learn to be persuasive and sell your sources on why they should give their time and experience to help you. This is somewhat like writing a query to an editor. You must project enthusiasm and tempt the source with your interesting idea for a story. If you have already queried your editor and received an expression of interest in the story, then tell this to your sources. Stress that you'd prefer to get the story from their company than one of their competitors.

The other approach to getting an interview is by sending

an introductory letter. I find this is time-consuming and not as successful as the telephone approach because it gives sources time to think up reasons why they should not grant the interview. In my letter I state my writing credentials, my experience, and my reasons for wanting an interview. If I have an assignment from an editor, I pass on this information as well. Included with the letter is a copy of the magazine for which I will be writing, or a copy of a published story of mine, to give an example of the way I do my work. I close my letter by saying that I will telephone on a certain day, usually in about a week's time, to set up the interview. I then make a notation on my desk calendar so that I place the call on the day specified.

* Get the interview
* Call ahead
* Give your name and credentials
* Explain why you want to interview that person
* Suggest a date.

Preparation for an interview should begin as soon as you decide to ask for one. When making the appointment for the interview mention the broad topic you will cover and explain that you will narrow this down during the interview. Tell your contact the kind of questions you anticipate asking so that he can prepare his responses and offer supporting material or evidence in writing at the actual interview. Even better, send a list if there is sufficient time before the interview takes place. It saves time for both of you. Any written observations provided by the sources can be paraphrased or used as direct quotes by you later on. They may provide you with an angle not covered at the time of the interview.

Step No. 4. How to Conduct the Interview

After an appointment is made, I compose a list of questions, usually a dozen. I put the most important questions at the top of my list. Towards the end of my prepared list I will repeat a key question, only this time rephrasing it in order that the source might respond from a different angle. More questions are asked when I conduct the interview based on the replies I receive.

I try to anticipate how the person will respond and I avoid

103

asking questions that may lead to a "yes" or "no" response. Using the format, "Can you tell me a little bit about how your company—promoted its new product—or—solved the problem of tardiness, or absenteeism,"—or—improved employee relations," I attempt to get the most coverage out of each question. I have the source tell me in his own words the problem he faced and how he solved it.

During the interview, dig deep for facts. Don't be satisfied with a one-sentence response. Rephrase your questions to help produce more details. Persist in asking, "How did you handle problem?" or "Let's go through that step by step, what did you do when . . .?" Always ask the source to tell you what happened in the end. "What were the results?" "How did the employees benefit from this?" and "How did the company benefit?" Remember, you can always cut back and omit some of this information when you prepare your final draft. It's better to ask too many questions than too few.

Filter out the puffery before you complete your story. Many businessmen, dealers, and salesmen whom you interview will not miss the opportunity to plug their own products, company or behavior. Screen their comments, select only the material that applies to your needs, and look for ideas and behavior that are beneficial and of interest to your readers.

I prefer to tape my interviews because I can transcribe the tapes days later and don't have to rely on my memory for direct quotes. Furthermore, the interview proceeds smoothly on a conversational level rather than inquisitional if I look at the subject instead of scribbling down his remarks in a notebook leaving him only the top of my head to talk to.

Occasionally you'll find a source who is not eloquent when it comes to describing his job. Here is where you have to do more than switch on the tape recorder, ask questions, and later transcribe the responses. You have to probe and help extract the story. As the writer of the story you should have an idea of the kind of information you want from that particular person. You can help the source articulate that information by careful questioning, rephrasing your questions and even suggesting that his experiences might be similar to a previous interview you had conducted. For example, you might say, "When you solved this problem did you find that

104

the employees responded more favorably to oral presentations rather than to written communications? When I interviewed the general manager of ----------- Company he said he did better with oral presentations." Having led the source to the type of comments you want him to make he is usually then able to take over. Another way I get my sources to open up is by saying to them, "Describe what you do in a typical day at work. Walk me through your day verbally." By using this method they are able to explain in their own words exactly what it is they do, and what are the problems they encounter. Then, I am able to zero in and aim specific questions as how they solve the problems.

Sweeping, broad generalizations are not wanted in business writing. You must be specific and give plenty of examples. When interviewing business and professional people the goal is to tell the readers exactly how your subjects did what they did, in detail. This is why you must narrow down to a specific topic.

When I received an assignment to do a story about employee morale during a company takeover, my editor suggested that "it's most helpful to know what supervisors can do to keep up their employees' morale." I therefore asked questions that concentrated on how supervisors could reassure their employees, prepare them for the takeover, and ensure that they continued to be productive employees during the period of transition.

The article was well received. "It's great to get a story on a topic off the beaten track for a change," the editor wrote. "So often, we seem to redo the same subjects over and over again. Your article is very thorough—has a lot of good material in it."

When conducting the interview
* Prepare a list of questions
* Avoid "yes" or "no" responses
* Ask source to state the problem encountered and the action taken
* Dig deep for facts
* Rephrase questions to improve response
* Look for ideas to help your readers.

Step No. 5. Putting the Article Together

I make it a point to send a thank-you letter to the person I interviewed within a day or two of the interview. While expressing my appreciation for the time and help given I also mention that I will send him a copy of the article after it is published. I believe this follow-up contact is good puhlic relations and the source will be receptive to granting another interview with me later on.

After transcribing my interview tapes I prepare an outline (See Outline for Articles) that ties in with the questions on my list. Business articles are very similar in composition to feature articles. They need a good, hard-hitting lead, usually describing the problem faced. The body details the steps taken to solve the problem. This must include statistics, facts, or anecdotes to back up what your source is saying. This is where you show and tell the reader that here are some suggestions worth considering. The conclusion is stated either in your source's words or else you draw a comparison between his findings and those given by other authorities.

Tidy up the poorly phrased statements and don't let your sources appear foolish or illiterate. Write and rewrite a number of drafts until you have produced a smoothly flowing story. Before typing the final copy I let my business sources see the draft of the story I have prepared. One market that publishes numerous business stories insists that their writers do this and that those people who have been interviewed should sign the draft as an indication that they have seen it. Some people return the draft without any comments while others include additional facts or statements. A few delete a sentence or two. Unless this action involves what I think to be a critical point, I don't object. I've found that getting signed approval for publication can work for me. By informing the interviewee that he will have the opportunity to see my story before it is sent to the editor he becomes receptive and easier to work with. Obtaining signed approval is a prerequisite only for the business interviews that I write up. When writing other feature stories I omit this step.

Type the final copy in double-spaced lines. (See Manuscript Preparation and Mailing.) Some trade bulletins prefer to receive copy typed with the shorter 35 character line, others

106

like to receive stories with a 70 character line, roughly ten words per line.

Always include a self-addressed stamped envelope with your manuscript submissions unless you are writing on assignment, in which case the editor will pay the postage for any correspondence.

Photographs

In addition to securing that all-important interview you may have to obtain photographs to accompany the story. You can either take your own photographs or alternatively, try to locate a free-lance photographer to work with you on a speculative basis. If the article and photographs are bought as a package deal by the editor you arrange for a split of the fee privately. Otherwise, pay the photographer the amount the editor gives you for the photograph. Remember, beginning photographers need credits as much as beginning writers. Another way to obtain photographs is by contacting the public relations department of the company you are interviewing. They are usually very willing to help out with photographs, especially if it means additional publicity for their company.

If you send photogaphs along with your story make sure you have a signed release in your possession. Many magazines require this, and it is easier to obtain permission when you conduct the interview and take the photographs than to have to return later on for a signature on a release form. Let the editor know what photographic credits should be given.

See also Interviewing
Outline for Articles
Photograph Releases

NEWS WRITING

"Newspapers are the world's mirrors."
— James Ellis

What is the difference between a news story and a feature? The first difference is the writing angle. A straight news story focuses on the facts whereas a feature focuses on the human interest angle of the facts. The second difference is length and timeliness. The news story is generally shorter in length and is timely; it is about things that are happening now or have just happened.

Richard Cole, Dean of the School of Journalism, at the University of North Carolina, explained the difference between the two types of writing this way. "News stories nearly always are based on some specific event that took place in the recent past. Either the writer just covered a meeting or watched a parade or interviewed a celebrity. The event may have a news angle that hinges on public affairs. It may be of general interest to the public, such as the budgetary process of government or any agency related to government, rather than what we call 'soft feature' news." Features have more to do with human interest, they are timeless stories that relate more to individuals rather than to policy or something of social significance, says Cole.

Cole says he has noticed a change in the direction of news stories. "More and more we are getting away from the billboard function and the event orientation and we are coming to have an issue orientation, that is, in-depth reporting about serious subjects."

On the local scene this in-depth reporting would apply to news stories covering the community perspective. Such questions as what is happening in the community, or analyses of happenings in other communities, make interesting topics for the local newspaper's readers. Names make news, too. Famous people visiting the area, local people who have received awards, or newly-elected to serve in community organizations,

108

even ordinary citizens in the spotlight because of tragedy or heroism, are good leads for news stories.

Construction of a New Story

Though the construction and content of news stories may be changing, says Cole, we are not getting away from the inverted pyramid style news report yet. "That will always be with us, but it's not as formal as it used to be. We have more feature-style leads, more descriptive leads. I think this is good because they are easier to read."

The inverted pyramid form that allows the shortening of a news story to be done by lopping-off the bottom paragraphs is not a natural way to write, said Cole. "It builds down instead of up. People have to be taught to do it, and I think it turns some readers off." When using the inverted pyramid style the writer places the summary up in the lead, after which the supporting details are given in inverted order of importance.

Remember the 5 W's and one H for the news lead. Include, "Who, What, Why, When, Where and How" in your lead so that readers will quickly identify the people, places, and events connected with the story. The body of the news story should merely expand on each of the points included in the lead in the same order and in greater detail.

News writing, although terse, must contain the best qualities to hold reader interest and to assure a clear understanding of the story. Words must be common and familiar, sentences compact, and paragraphs rarely more than six standard typewritten lines. Objectivity must be used when writing the news story. Attribute the source, when possible. Do not include opinions unless you are writing an editorial or take the precaution to inform readers that this is your own point of view. In the words of Daniel R. Williamson, "Opinions and fiction are expressly banned from all but special sections of the newspaper. The editorial page, of course, provides outlet for opinions and it is clearly labeled as opinionated material."

In order to establish continuity in style, capitalization, abbreviation, punctuation, and spelling, most newspapers follow the guidelines set down in the Associated Press or United Press International style books.

It is easier to place a feature story than a news story with a newspaper, but if you have access to information that would make a public affairs story, then by all means contact the city editor of your local and regional newspapers.

Two well-known reference sources for newspaper information are the *Directory of Newspapers and Periodicals*, published by N. W. Ayer and Son, and *The Editor and Publisher Yearbook*, both available at most libraries. The latter also includes information on syndicates and news services and picture and press services.

See also Syndication

OUTLINE FOR ARTICLES

Journalists and nonfiction writers must learn to write to space; that is to write their story in the number of words allowed by the editor. Otherwise they will have to do a great deal of rewriting to satisfy the editor's space allotment. It is inefficient for a writer to prepare 3000 words when only 1500 are called for. Far better that you should set out to write 1500 and no more. It will take you less time to prepare your stories and consequently you'll be able to turn out more.

It is often helpful to prepare a worksheet in advance, indicating the approximate number of words you think necessary for each section of the story. I use Walter S. Campbell's method of assigning an approximate number of words to each part of the "HEY YOU SEE SO" formula that is given in the section Formula for Features in this book.

Here is an outline I prepared for an article called "Decorate With Shells." By using Campbell's formula, I projected the total number of words needed would be 1700. This is how I divided that number into the various parts of the story:

50 Words — HEY

The introduction to the story. Get the reader into mood. Write about the end of summer when back at home with your beach finds. What can you do with them? Don't put in a drawer or shoe box. Instead. . .

150 Words — YOU

Maintains reader interest. Point out beauty of shells, compare them to jewelry. Provide brief description of how they were used in the past as money, decoration, and token of a religious pilgrimage.

1320 Words — SEE

Describe how other people have decorated with shells, made collages, figurines, and picture displays. Add comments

111

from shell experts and cite authors of books on shell art. Suggest ways in which readers might use shells for decoration, the last example being my tips on how to display shells in glycerin.

200 Words — (First part) Decorating with shells
400 Words — (Second part) Collages, displays, and jewelry
600 Words — (Third part) How to assemble displays
120 Words — (Fourth part) My tips on shells in glycerin.

180 Words — SO

Conclusion of article. Alludes again to the beach and reminds the reader of the beginning of the story. "As you get deeper into the field of conchology you may find yourself embarked on a lifelong hobby. . .and all it took was a trip to the beach."

Illustrate article with black and white photographs showing shell art displays etcetera.

Such a worksheet enables you to construct your article on sound principles, emphasizing what requires emphasis and slighting what does not. In this way you allot beforehand the approximate number of words which will be required to effectively present each item in your article. You will then have to consider what your transitions must be from case to case and how you will tie the whole thing together.

It is easy to know whether you are exceeding the number of words in each section if you know how many words are on an average page of your typing. I usually type 250 words to the page, so a story as outlined above should run just under seven pages of typing. Referring to my outline during the preparation of my rough draft I can see that my introductory lead HEY should be no longer than a quarter of a page, at the most a paragraph or two. The second part, YOU, is about three times as long as the lead. The bulk of the article consisting of the four examples, SEE, should run to almost five typewritten pages. The conclusion will take up about three-quarters of a page. Total = 6-3/4 pages or 1700 words.

A certain amount of overwriting does occur. Knowing ahead that I must restrict the length of the lead to no more than a quarter of a page I would not prepare a two-page lead. Try this method and see for yourself how much easier it is to prepare articles and essays when you limit beforehand the number of words you will write. It takes some practice and the ability to condense material, but writing to space is a must for newspaper reporters and columnists. It is good discipline for article writers as well.

See also Formula for Features
Know What You Want to Say

PAYMENT ON ACCEPTANCE OR ON PUBLICATION

Sell your work for payment on acceptance instead of on publication whenever possible. Time and again you will hear professional free-lance writers warn about the pitfalls of waiting for payment until after the story is published. So much can go wrong with payment on publication. You may wait months or years before your story gets published. The magazine may suspend or cease publishing before it gets to your story. It may go out of business after your story has been published but before you have been paid. In this case there's a good chance that your request for payment will be ignored. Another thing that can happen to a story accepted but not yet published is that it may be put aside or rejected because of a change in editorial policy.

As a professional you can't afford to wait for your money until the publication day rolls around. You should be paid promptly for the work you have done. That's the way I work with my trade journal editors, most of which pay me within two weeks after they receive my story, even though publication may not take place for six months or more.

The Choice is Yours

Before submitting your manuscripts learn which method of payment the publisher uses. Most market listings indicate whether payment is on acceptance or on publication or, worse, in contributor's copies. If a listing avoids any mention of payment it is an indication to me that there may not be a standard policy. I suggest you write to ask about rates before submitting any work to markets which are vague about payment. It may be that the magazine has omitted mentioning rates because it is a new publication and the publisher is waiting to see how subscriptions and sales progress before making any commitments to contributing writers.

Some magazines pay only when they have to. When a writer submits material without asking about terms beforehand, the publication may not feel bound to make any

114

payment at all even if they publish the feature. Without a commitment in writing you have no recourse for filing a nonpayment claim.

You should also know that some publications use a varying payment scale whereby new writers breaking into that market for the first time get paid a lower amount than regular contributors. If you progress to making repeat sales to a market and feel you should be paid more than the rate for your first submissions, then write and ask for an increase. You may get it, or at least an encouraging letter that states you will be considered for an increase later because the magazine still wants to receive your material. The choice of further sales to this market is yours.

I think it is better to make a sale at a lower rate of pay to the publication that pays on acceptance rather than to accept a precarious promise for more money from a market that pays on or after publication. The key word is publication. Remember, you only get paid if the story is published.

An experience that I had some years ago will demonstrate why payment on publication is so unsatisfactory. It began back in November, 1975 when I sent a feature article to a specialty magazine that was listed as seeking stories on animals and pet care. It was my first submission to this market and I sent a self-addressed stamped envelope with my cover letter so that the manuscript could be returned if it was rejected.

I waited two months before sending a friendly inquiry asking if they had any word for me about the manuscript. The reply came by return mail. They liked the interview very much and planned to use it in their 1976 Summer issue. I was willing to wait the additional six months until publication and considered the story sold.

In early Summer, 1976 I wrote again. This time I asked if the article had been published and would they please send several copies for my files along with the check. There was no response. However, to my dismay I read a report that another free-lance writer was still waiting to be paid by this market for a story published some six months earlier. That doesn't bode well for my story, I thought. Nevertheless, I waited until October before writing once again to ask if my article had

115

been published. Only this time I requested that if they didn't intend to use the story shortly they should return it to me so that I could submit it elsewhere. Once again I enclosed an SASE with my letter. Additionally, I sent the letter by certified mail, Signature Receipt Requested, so that I would have evidence that my request for return of the manuscript had been received and by whom.

My letter crossed in the mail with one from the magazine staff in which they informed me that they had decided to delay publishing the article until the following summer (1977). By now I was beginning to doubt whether I wanted to try to locate another market. I felt I had invested enough time and postage with this one, and so I stretched my patience a little bit more and replied that I'd agree to the story being held for 1977. However, in view of my long wait I asked to be paid in advance of publication. It took another two months before I got a response in December 1976. They only paid on publication, but would return my story if I wanted to submit it to another magazine.

In retrospect I realize I should never have allowed the situation to drag on this way, but back in December 1976 I was less experienced. I gave my permission for payment and publication to be delayed until the summer of 1977.

Now, if you think this story has a happy ending you'll be disappointed just as I was. Stick around and I'll relate how they delivered the coup de grâce.

Several weeks after the magazine's offer to return my story if I didn't want to wait for payment, I received a form letter to the point that beginning with the next issue the magazine would be under a new editorial direction. The staff had been asked to return all manuscripts currently on file to their authors. Even more galling, the form letter ended with the invitation, "Please feel free to submit material in the future if it is very specifically health-related and is accompanied by black and white glossy prints."

What's this, I thought? My feature fit completely into that category yet they were going to return it to me just so that I could resubmit it. Not a chance! Fourteen months had elapsed from the time of submission, through acceptance, and finally to rejection, and all I had to show for my effort was a thick correspondence file and request to resubmit it. If I learned anything at all from that fruitless experience it was one should be suspicious of any publication that procrastinates in accepting manuscripts or is negligent in responding to inquiries. Had I heeded the storm warning sent up by that other free-lancer, I could have saved at least six months of anguish.

When I received the returned manuscript I didn't have the motivation to start making the rounds with it. I felt the story had possibilities but needed updating with new material. Somehow, I never got around to revising it. I've lost interest in that subject and gone on to others that I find more exciting to write about for editors who are more fair and more business-like.

See Kill Fees
Market Listings
Selling Your Writing

PHOTOGRAPH RELEASES

When taking photographs you must be careful not to invade the privacy of others or trespass on their right to be left alone. It is to your advantage to routinely obtain a model release whenever you are taking photographs. The model release is a consent form permitting the photographer to take or use photographs and should be signed by the person being photographed. If you are photographing a minor the release must be signed by a parent or guardian of the minor. Since many states have laws which forbid a name or picture from being used for commercial purposes without the subject's authorization the release protects you against possible suits for invasion of privacy or legal damages.

Most magazines and newspapers do not require releases on photographs to be used strictly for editorial illustrations. Such photographs which are truthful representations of an actual event usually fall within the news publication's privilege to publish. However, a model release is required from all recognizable persons in a picture which is to be used for advertising purposes. This includes photographs appearing in brochures, leaflets, or industrial publications, that can be remotely considered published for commercial purposes.

The short release form that I use covers most photographic assignments and takes little time for the subject to read and sign. It reads thus:

In consideration for value received, receipt of which is hereby acknowledged, I hereby consent that the photographs taken of me in whole or in part, or any reproduction of the same may be used by_____ or by others with the consent of _____ for the purpose of illustration, advertising, trade, or publication in any manner, and I also consent to the use of my name in connection therewith.

Signature

Date Name

Witness Address

118

Let me explain about the words "value received." You are not required to pay the subject to sign the agreement. The "value received" may be as high as a professional model's fee or as little as one dollar, or simply the subject's gratification in seeing her photograph published.

For photographing a minor here is an example of the release you might use:

> I hereby affirm that I am the parent (guardian) of _____ and without further consideration I hereby irrevocably consent that each of the photographs which have been taken of him/her by _____ and/or his assigns may be used for advertising, trade, illustration, or publication in any manner.

> Date   Signature
>   Name
>   Address

Never send your original model release along with a photograph—copy it, and keep the original release in your files.

If you want to know more about the business end of photography, a helpful booklet, "Business Practices in Photography," has been published by ASMP (The Society of Photographers in Communication), 60 E. 42nd Street, New York, NY 10017. There is a charge of $5 for the booklet.

See also Legal Information for the Writer

119

PHOTOJOURNALISM

Photojournalism combines photographic skills with writing and graphics. Photojournalists are in growing demand, says Robert L. Kerns, author of *Photojournalism: Photography With a Purpose.*

Most free-lance writers know the importance of photographs. Pictures can make a good article better and they can persuade an editor to purchase borderline manuscripts that might otherwise be rejected. Photographs can add life and excitement to text. Many an article would never have seen print had it not been for some well-chosen illustrations.

If you wish to become a photojournalist you must learn how to handle the mechanics of a camera without thinking. Then you are free to devote all your thinking to composing and getting good pictures that tell the story with honesty and impact. Taking a course in photography will provide the background, but familiarity and ease with your camera and subjects is achieved only by practice.

In his book, Kerns describes basic camera techniques and provides instruction and assignments to help you put into practice the points covered. The more you do, the better prepared you will become. Although written primarily for classroom instruction, this book can be used by individuals who wish to develop successful photographic habits. Helpful advice on choosing a camera and equipment is also provided. Start off by using a 35 mm camera, said Kerns. "This is popular among photojournalists because it is small, extremely mobile, highly versatile, and produces pictures of the utmost technical excellence." You should master the use of the normal lens (45 to 58 mm) before considering other focal lengths such as wide-angle, or telephoto lenses, he said.

Taking Pictures

Many inexperienced photojournalists try to include too much in the picture. The reason for this, according to Kerns, is that they are not sure what they want to say or are too timid to get close enough to the subject to say it. "Show what is needed, but nothing more." If the picture is not totally clear, explain in the cutlines or captions. A caption is a heading placed over the picture; the cutline, or underline, refers to the descriptive lines beneath or at the side of the picture.

Carry a small notebook with you for writing down the names of people you photograph, the location, and what's going on. Do this before you leave the scene of the photograph. You may not have time to go back the next day to ask who's who. Always take along a couple of model release forms in case these are needed. If you are covering a news event it's imperative that you come back with all the facts or your photographs will have little value.

Identifying Photographs and Slides

Never mail out photographs without identifying the source and subject. On the back, place your name and address, the subject's name, or negative file number. I use a rubber stamp, lightly inked for placing my name and address on my photographs. The pressure of the stamp does not affect the front of the print, whereas ballpoint pen, and even pencil, may.

To identify color transparencies I type my name, address, and slide number on small press-on labels and place them onto the cardboard mount of the slide. On a sheet of paper I type the slide number corresponding to the ones I am sending out and list more detailed information such as where the slide was taken, the name of the event, or the names of the subjects and what they are doing.

Market Information for Photojournalists

The smaller circulation magazines are a great market for manuscript-photograph packages. But the larger markets shouldn't be overlooked either, especially if you have an extra-fine picture.

Market information can be found in *The Artist's & Photographer's Market*, published by Writer's Digest, and the *Gebbie Directory of House Organ Magazines*, published by House Magazine Publishing Company, Inc., Sioux City, Iowa. Each directory provides specific information about thousands of

121

publications, including the editor's name, editorial requirements, rates, conditions of payment, and special requirements. A few markets insist on color transparencies being 2-1/4 x 2-1/2 inch or larger, but the 35 mm transparency is now almost universally accepted. Most markets consider color prints not acceptable. Black and white prints should be 8 x 10 inch in size, either high-gloss or on smooth stock.

When mailing photographs or transparencies protect them by placing them between two corrugated boards and bind with two rubber bands stretched from corner to corner. Do not bend or fold. When mailing color transparencies I like to use the commercially available plastic sheets (8-1/2 x 11 inch) that hold up to 20 slides in individual pockets. Again, I protect the sheets by inserting them between corrugated boards.

Follow the same rules for mailing photographs that you use for mailing manuscripts. (See section on Manuscript Preparation and Mailing.) Use a large enough envelope to avoid bending and always include a self-addressed stamped envelope for return of your submissions.

The following magazines provide information about markets, photographic techniques, treatment, and contests.

Industrial Photographer, United Business Publications, Inc., 475 Park Avenue, New York, NY 10016

Photo Contest News, Box 1269 Glendora, CA 91740

Photomethods, Ziff-Davis Publishing Co., 1 Park Avenue, New York, NY 10016

The Professional Photographer, PPA Publications and Events, Inc., 1090 Executive Way, Des Plaines, IL 60018

The Rangefinder, 1312 Lincoln Blvd., Santa Monica, CA 90406.

See also Photograph Releases

POETRY

Writing poetry is a very popular activity and you can make money at it. More entries are received in the poetry category of writing contests than in any other category, the Director of a writers' conference told me. "For every feature article we receive ten poems," she said. She attributed the high number of poetry entries to the saleability of feature articles. Many feature writers keep their manuscripts circulating in the mail or they sell all they can produce. The poet always has something at hand, either written down or in her head. Unfortunately, poetry is not generally a money-making endeavor.

There are some magazines that purchase serious and humorous verse, but the commercial outlets for poetry are limited in number. Nevertheless, nonpaying markets do offer poets a forum for their work and should be seriously considered. Getting your work published, even without pay, is better than never publishing. Literary magazines are open to poetry submissions and usually pay in contributor's copies, prizes, or awards. There is also the possibility that your poem may be selected for an anthology. Writing credits should always be used when you contact a paying market.

Poetry market lists of large-circulation magazines, college, and literary magazines, as well as greeting card markets, appear every March in *The Writer* magazine. You might also purchase a copy of *The International Directory of Little Magazines and Small Presses*, published annually by Dustbooks, P.O. Box 1056, Paradise, CA 95969. This is another market reference book designed to help you save time in getting published. Arranged alphabetically, the candid, thumbnail sketches will help you locate the smaller publishers who are interested in off-beat or avant-garde material but who are not listed in the *Writer's Market* or *Literary Market Place.*

One avenue for sales for those who write verse is the greeting card market. It is a lucrative market, although tough to break into. One card company specializing in humorous contemporary cards buys 600 to 800 ideas a year from a submission of 4000 to 5000 ideas a week. According to one manufacturer, the reason most greeting card submissions fail is that they are either not funny enough or they do not put across a thought or message suitable for a greeting card. Greeting cards can be conventional, inspirational, informal, juvenile, humorous, or studio. All, however, convey a "from me to you" message. The message must be expressed in one or two lines or short verse.

Standard payment is from $25 to $50 per card idea and $1 to $3 per line for verse, reports Walter G. Olesky, in *1,000 Tested Money-Making Markets for Writers.* Unless you are an accomplished artist don't send a drawing with your idea because most greeting card companies use their own staff artists to illustrate the cards.

Information on names, addresses, and editorial guidelines of greeting card companies has been assembled in a free booklet, *Artists and Writers Market List,* by the National Association of Greeting Card Publishers. To obtain this booklet send a self-addressed stamped envelope to the Associatiion at 600 Pennsylvania Avenue, S.E. No.300, Washington, DC 20003.

How to Submit Poetry and Greeting Card Verse

When submitting poetry to magazines, use a standard 8-1/2 x 11 inch sheet of typing paper with no more than one poem on each page. Type your name and address on each page. Most editors prefer to see only a few samples at a time. As in the case of other submissions, your poems will only be returned if a SASE is enclosed.

When submitting material to greeting card companies type your verse on cards. Guidelines offered by The National Association of Greeting Card Publishers indicate that verse and messages should be typed double-spaced on a 3 x 5 or 4 x 6 inch card, one verse or message on each card. Use only one side of the card. Put your name and address in the upper left-hand corner. Do not send out more than ten verses or ideas in a group to any one publisher.

Contests, Awards, and Fellowships

To help make up for the lack of commercial outlets there are numerous poetry contests you can enter. Here are three that I know of:

Carolina Quarterly Fiction-Poetry Contest, Greenlaw Hall 066-A, University of North Carolina, Chapel Hill, NC 27514. Poetry awards: $150 for first, $100 second and $50 third place. No limit to length. Open to poets who have not published a book-length manuscript.

The National Writers Club holds an annual poetry writing competition for its members. Entries must be unpublished and not exceed 60 lines. All types of poems are eligible; lyric, ballad, free verse, experimental, conventional. For further information on entry fee and deadline, write: The National Writers Club, 1450 S. Havana, Aurora, CO 80012. Cash awards for the 1980 contest ran as high as $200 for first prize, $100 for second, $50 for third, and down to $10 for the 5th-10th prize.

The Writer's Digest Creative Writing Contest includes a category for poems of no longer than 16 lines. They must be original, unpublished, and not previously submitted to a Writer's Digest contest. Announcements of the yearly contest appear in *Writer's Digest* magazines, January through July.

Many contests do not return entries after the competition is over, so always keep a copy of any material you submit.

The Writer's Handbook and *The Writer's Market* both publish lists of contests and awards. In addition, current announcements of literary prizes, awards, and fellowships are given every month in *The Writer*, together with names and addresses of whom to contact and the deadlines for entry or application.

After you have established yourself as a published poet you may be eligible for special funding. Find out if your state or county has a Literary and Arts Council that supports the creative endeavors of writers and artists. The North Carolina Arts Council, for example, awards four fellowships each year, (generally in the amount of $5,000) to allow the recipients to set aside time, purchase supplies and materials, or achieve specific career goals. There are special requirements that applicants must be able to meet. They must be able to

125

document that they have a minimum of five years of professional-level experience in their art form and that they have been a resident of North Carolina for at least one year immediately prior to making application. Applications will be accepted from poets, fiction writers, playwrights, composers, and choreographers during odd-numbered years. Application deadline is June 1. For further information contact the Literary Arts Coordinator, North Carolina Arts Council, Department of Cultural Resources, Raleigh, NC 27611.

See also Conferences, Clubs, and Contests

PUBLICITY FOR CLUBS AND ORGANIZATIONS

Another way of getting your words into print is to volunteer your services to prepare publicity releases for local clubs and community service organizations. This is an excellent avenue for making contact with the news media. Even though you may not get paid for your work you will have more clippings for your writing credit file and it is quite possible that the contacts you make with local newspaper, radio, and television personnel may help you to obtain other writing assignments.

To get started you'll need to know the publicity goals of the club or organization. After you've made the initial contact with the organization and established that they want your help you should then schedule a meeting with the officers and find out what they expect from a publicity campaign. With whom will you be working? Is there one person who will pass information on to you or are there several, each in charge of a special project? How are you assured that the necessary information will get to you? These and similar questions should be discussed at the meeting.

Publicity Calendar

Plan your publicity strategy with the aid of a calendar. This will be your basic plan of attack. On the calendar, note the dates of meetings, special events, elections, and anything else of importance to the organization that may need publicizing. Then mark ahead of these events the deadlines for sending out news releases and radio and television announcements.

Follow the three E's — Explore, Explain, Expand

Explore all angles. Try to find the most important, unique, or interesting fact about what you are publicizing and build your story around that. For example, is the speaker famous, local, or from out-of-town? Is the club or organization doing something unusual? A breakfast meeting? A project with the

127

public schools or local historical society that might be of interest to the local community? A benefit for an individual and why? Is the group touring a facility or donating something to the local hospital?

Explain fully. Be sure to include all necessary facts in your story—what, when, who, where, and why.

Expand your use of the media. Don't rely completely on any one medium for publicity. Think of how you can best present your information to radio, TV, and the newspapers. Read your newspaper thoroughly, find out what kind of sections it has during the week and on Sundays, and who writes them. Watch and listen to local TV and radio stations, find out what kind of special programming they have — talk shows, farm programs, calendars.

Is there more than one angle? For example, if the speaker is a prize-winning flower arranger don't just send an article to the newspaper announcing the meeting; contact and invite the garden editor to attend. Find out if a TV or radio talk show may be interested in an interview, but always check with speakers before arranging anything extra for them.

Making Contacts

Before you begin writing stories you need to locate your news media contacts, that is the individuals with whom you will be working on a regular basis. For example, to obtain newspaper publicity, an announcement about arts or entertainment events should be sent to the arts reporters, if the newspaper has one. Business organization news should go to the business editor. Public service projects, that aid local children, for example, might be of interest to the city editor. Women's club news is normally handled by the women's page editor. Some newspapers now call this section the "Style" or "Living" section.

Call your local radio and television stations and find out if you should send your stories to the public affairs director or someone else. Get that person's name.

Do be sure that you are the only person from the organization that you represent that is working with the news media on these subjects. Duplication of effort is a waste of time for everyone concerned and can lead to problems.

128

Below is a checklist of the basic points to follow when preparing newspaper, radio, and TV releases:

* Put your name, address, phone number and the name of the organization on each article.
* Put the current date and the date the article is to be released. If your story is to be released on receipt, then put "For Immediate Release." If you are sending an advance story (installation of officers) your story should be marked for release on a specific date. Most editors will try to comply with your request.
* Remember the deadlines established by each editor and don't break them.
* If the article or news item is for a special program or column then be sure to indicate this on your copy.
* Find out how each editor wants his or her copy prepared and stick to this method. (Most newspaper editors want double-spaced copy, typed on one side of letter-sized paper; but check this out.)
* Double-check the spelling of all names. Specify dates (Sunday, December 2, not "next Sunday").
* Be brief: Use whole sentences and paragraphs that contain all necessary information. What, when, who, where, why—but no padding or unnecessary words, especially adjectives.
* Make machine, not carbon, copies if you are sending out multiple releases. Keep one copy for your files. If they want it, make an extra for the organization.

Broadcast Tips
* Most stations appreciate receiving information at least two weeks in advance of the date the announcement should be running. (If your story is about an upcoming lecture on November 1, send your public service spot announcement to your contact at the station during the first week in October. Most stations will run your announcement for no more than one week so clearly indicate at the top of the page the dates you would like the spot broadcast: FOR BROADCAST OCT. 28—NOV. 1.)

* Keep your announcement short, about 15 to 30 seconds in timed length. Time is everything in radio and television so when requesting free time, it is a good idea to measure your words. A 10-second spot for radio will include about 25 words; a 20-second spot, 50 words; and a 60-second spot, 150 words.
* Use short sentences that are easy to read. Practice reading your announcement aloud. If it "flows" you have a well-written release.
* All public service spot announcements should be typed in capital letters. Write out all numbers except times and dates (ON SEPTEMBER 30 at 8 P.M.). If an organization is known by an abbreviation, type dashes between each letter (Y-M-C-A or N-A-A-C-P). Give the phonetic spelling for names which may be difficult to pronounce in parentheses.
* On the outside of the envelope, in the lower left corner, clearly print PUBLIC SERVICE SPOT ANNOUNCE-MENT. Labelled like this, your announcement should get to the right person immediately.

Television Tips
* For television public service spot announcements, follow the same tips suggested for radio with this exception: If slides and photographs (video) are used, the TV broadcaster will read slower. In other words, audio slows down so that a 10-second spot is 15 words, and a 60-second spot, 120 words. Video should change about every 10 seconds on public service spot announcements for television.

(Portions of the above material appeared in the handbook, *Explore, Explain, Expand*, published by the North Carolina Triangle Chapter of Women in Communications, Inc., and are reproduced by kind permission.)

After you've mastered the handling of publicity for local clubs and ommunity service organizations you can then take your published clippings to local business markets such as art galleries, automobile dealers, health clubs, and restaurants, and offer to write promotional copy about their businesses. As a

130

further step, you should contact the public relations and advertising agencies in your area and ask if they need rush-time help to prepare brochures, public service campaigns, speeches, television or radio commercials. You may find, as did one of my friends, that you can acquire sufficient paying clients with your promotional writing to provide you with a regular income.

See also Ghostwriting

QUERY LETTERS AND OUTLINES

Why query before you write? Why can't you write first and then try to sell? If you are writing fiction of course you'll write the story before you look for a buyer. To sell nonfiction articles professionals query first and write only when an interested editor has been located. Many publications today refuse to read unsolicited manuscripts. The editors only want to see queries. Queries save time for both the editor and the writer. That's why it is so important for you to query before commiting time and money to paper.

The trick in querying is to give just enough information to whet the editor's appetite so that he or she wants to see the finished piece. Two kinds of queries are commonly used, the informal letter and the more detailed outline. After a while you will find out which one works best for you and which your editor prefers.

Get to the point at once. Tell exactly what you propose to do, and what will be your point of view. If you have any special qualifications to write such an article mention them. If you are a beginning writer do not say so. What you lack in writing experience may be compensated for by offering the editor a new slant on an old subject. Give the names of your sources, or the references you will use to substantiate the query. How many words will you submit? Your query should tell the editor everything in brief that he needs to know to make a decision. Above all, be enthusiastic about your idea. Focus on the importance, eccentricity, or humor of the article. Close by telling how long you will take to produce a completed manuscript after the editor has given you the go-ahead.

Make only one proposal per letter. Most editors prefer to consider one idea from a writer at a time, particularly if they have never worked with that writer before. They don't know if the writer will produce what is promised.

Receptive Editors

When editors appear receptive to your work and tell you that they would like to see more of it, listen to what they are saying. Followup with more queries.

Not so long ago, after making an initial sale to one magazine, an upcoming trip to Seattle prompted me to make a telephone query to the magazine in order to find out if the editor was interested in a travel feature on that city. Because of the time element, I had to know immediately whether my proposal would be acceptable to that publication. An assistant editor gave me an affirmative response and, upon my return from Seattle, I confirmed in writing that I would be submitting the story to them. I sent it in as promised, made another sale, and received an encouraging note, "Look forward to more." In 12 months this market bought four feature articles from me.

Confirm in Writing

Put your proposal in writing even if you already have a verbal go-ahead from the editor. I sent the following confirmation to an editor I had met at a writers conference several years ago:

Dear Mr. ------------:

This is to confirm our conversation at the North Carolina Writers Conference last Saturday during which you expressed an interest in receiving a feature article on the topic of seashells.

As discussed, I will send you, early in January, a feature for your Outer Banks edition to be published in the summer. Approximately 1500 to 2000 words, it will be tied in with the Outer Banks angle, discuss which areas are good for shelling, and tell readers "how to do it," including how to clean and display their finds. I would also mention the North Carolina Shell club and include some remarks from the members on how they got started on this fascinating hobby.

A selection of black and white photographs and color transparencies will accompany the feature.

133

You said that payment for this type of feature would be about $-------- and that is acceptable to me.

Yours sincerely,

Rita Berman

In this acceptance letter I spelled out when I would submit the feature, the approximate length, what it would cover, how it would tie in with the magazine's special edition, and that it would be illustrated by photographs and transparencies. I also confirmed that the fee we discussed was acceptable.

The response from the editor was enthusiastic; he wanted more. After you've done business with an editor and your writing has been satisfactory you won't need to sell yourself with every query. I handle these follow-up queries by making reference to my previous article that they published. That removes me from the "unknown" category. To one editor I wrote:

Dear Mr.-------------:
You may recall you published one of my articles, "USA Sales" in ----------- January, 1974, and I later queried you on a piece about Jamaica without success.

This summer my husband and I are visiting Grand Cayman Island for a shell-collecting vacation. I wonder if you would be interested in an article on real estate opportunities in the Cayman Islands, prices of homes, amenities, etc.?

I enclose a couple of International Reply Coupons and look forward to your reply.

Yours sincerely,

Rita Berman

Because the market was an overseas one I enclosed International Reply Coupons, not an SASE with my letter.

The editor's response to my query letter was to send a clipping of an article he had published some 18 months earlier and to say "we would be interested in a further piece about the estate opportunities in the islands, prices of homes, amenities, etc., written from your point of view and I would be very happy to see an article with photographs."

Establish your professionalism by showing that you can meet your deadlines and turn in manuscripts that live up to your queries. Don't promise more than you can deliver.

Query Outlines

The brief, informal letter works well with a simple subject and most times is all that is needed. Occasionally an editor will specify that he wants to see an outline. An outline may be from one to two pages in length. It should offer detailed information about the material you will include and should show the editor that you have thought out exactly what you will be writing. You might start off your outline with an anecdote or the lead beginning of the article to show the editor your writing style and pace, as Martha Monigle did in her outline query for "How to Name the Mother-in-Law," reprinted below by kind permission. Monigle received a go-ahead "on speculation" from *Modern Bride* on July 20, 1974, on her eleventh try to women's magazines. A $200 acceptance check arrived August 14, 1974 and the article appeared in the August/September 1978 issue of *Modern Bride.*

Martha Monigle   Article Query
P.O. Box 9181
Treasure Island, FL 33740

WHAT TO NAME THE MOTHER-IN-LAW

What to name the mother-in-law creates an odd game that young couples play.

"Your mother phoned today," the bride begins the game.

"Your mother?" he repeats. After a day at the

office, he wants a quiet martini.

"I can't call her Mrs. Davis when I'm Mrs. Davis. And she's not my mother."

"So call her Mom, or Mama, just like I do."

"That's too informal."

In turn, the groom's hackles rise if he's on the opposite side of that name-dodging board.

Lucky females and males in primitive societies had rules established by tradition. Brides in Siberia and certain parts of South America were ordered never to speak to their mothers-in-law nor to face them at any time. Furthermore, because the bride usually lived in the rear of the mother-in-law's house, she had to obey the custom of using a different and private entrance while being concealed in a long cloak.

*****

This 1000-word article will continue with a light approach to one aspect of the mother-in-law situation.

Authorities, such as Dr. Robert Briffault, author of *The Mothers*, will be quoted as well as the columnist, Ann Landers. Humorous anecdotes about coping with mothers-in-law by speech or letters will be related with examples of compromises reached by some ingenious couples. How this social title used to be settled with the birth of the first grandchild. Article will end with suggestions on solving this social problem.

As a freelance writer, I feel qualified to write this article.

In contrast to Monigle's free-flowing descriptive style my business outlines are more formal. Here's one outline that sold on its third time out. I received a go-ahead assignment in April, 1976, completed the story in May. It was accepted July and proofs were mailed to me in August. The story appeared in October in *Administrative Management* and I received a check for $60 in November, 1976. Receiving page proofs before publication is uncommon but this was a topline glossy magazine and it was their normal practice to send the writer page proofs to correct.

Rita Berman   Approximately 1500 words

INCENTIVE SCHEME PAYS OFF

"The reasons for adopting our Service Suggestion system were we sought to promote better office efficiency and we wanted to improve service to our customers, the subscribers of our health service plan," said Mr. -----------, treasurer and executive officer of ------------------ of North Carolina.

An average of 35 suggestions are turned in each month from the 1150 employees, and ----------- who serves as chairman of the Service Suggestion Committee told me that besides saving the company money, "It encourages our employees to do their jobs better, to think about their jobs, and they get a cash award for approved suggestions."

Both ---------- and -----------, coordinator of the program, have given me permission to write up their remarks into a case history for your readers.

Utilizing the problem-solution-results format, the article would cover why ---------- believes formal incentive schemes are helpful, how the ---------- scheme was begun, the objectives of the program, why a committee is more effective than relying on one or two people to review the suggestions, how the committee functions and examples of suggestions submitted and implemented. A brief mention of why some suggestions are turned down is also appropriate.

I would close with a description of how the incentive scheme pays off financially for management and employees, besides increasing employee morale and interest, and producing some unexpect-

137

ed benefits. "It's a healthy situation," says ------------
"after a suggestion has been accepted and an award
given we notice an increase in the number of new
suggestions made."

Along with my outline I sent a cover letter in which I
cited the names of well-known business publications that had
published my interviews and articles. Because the magazine
that I was querying was not available on newsstands I asked
for a free sample copy so that I could see the style of writing
that was preferred.

How Soon Will You Hear From the Editor?

I've found that most editors respond within two weeks if
they are interested in my proposal. Some never respond. One
editor waited a whole year before replying to my query and
then asked, "Can we have it within a month?" Occasionally,
an editor may express an interest in an idea but decline
because of overstocking, or because they have recently published or plan to publish something similar. In this instance if
you don't sell the story within the next six months I'd
suggest you query the editor again. Maybe he'll need more
material when your followup letter arrives.

Queries Are An Example of Your Writing

The editor will look at your query as an example of your
writing. Prepare a rough draft, edit it, rewrite it, and go over
it again until it is as snappy and appealing as you can make it.
Then send it off with a self-addressed stamped envelope for
the editor's reply.

Be sure to keep a copy of the query letter or outline. If
you are sending out a number of queries you might find it
useful to make a record on a 3 x 5 inch card for each query
sent out. List the date the query was sent off, the title of the
proposal, the market to which you sent it. Once a month, flip
through the cards to see which queries need to be resubmitted
to another publication.

I usually make a list of the markets that I plan to query
for each idea and note this on the card. If I draw a rejection
from the first market then I send the query out again to the

second name on the list, and to the third, and so on down the line until I receive a positive response from an editor. By making it a routine procedure to work through the list, I avoid being discouraged if my query is turned down by the first market.

How to query:

* Informal letter — one to two pages
* Detailed outline — one to two pages
* Offer only one idea at a time
* Prepare with care
* Always enclose an SASE or International Reply Coupon
* Don't give up on queries that have been rejected.
   Offer to other markets.

See also Editors Responses
Market Listings

REJECTIONS — HOW TO AVOID

The surefire way of avoiding rejections is to never send out any of your stories or articles. Just let them accumulate in your desk drawer and you will protect your ego and save yourself from the pangs of disappointment and despair. However, this behavior is non-productive because there are opportunities for having your work published and you'll never know about them. Assuming that your intentions are to join the ranks of published writers, the only way you can reach this goal is by exposing your writing to the critical gaze of editors and publishers. For most writers this entails living with rejection slips. Some joke about it, saying they intend to paper their walls with the slips. Others shrug off rejection slips easily and continue with writing. Many beginning writers abandon their dreams after receiving their first rejection slip. If you feel upset and distressed by rejection slips take comfort in the fact that you are not alone. When I first started free-lancing, I used to be unable to continue writing on the days that I learned an article of mine had been turned down. Sometimes I took several days to get my confidence up so that I could tackle that piece again and send it out, or try my hand at something different. However, I now know that the best way to overcome despair is to get right back at my desk, send out the manuscript to the next name on my marketing list and then continue with other projects.

To make a marketing list, I select three or four possible markets, number them in order of what appears to me to be the best prospects for a sale, send the manuscript to the publication at the top of the list, and place the list in my file together with a copy of the manuscript. Although most of my manuscripts are not written until I have received an assignment or a go-ahead response in reply to a query letter, there are occasions when I might prepare a manuscript for a market that doesn't insist on seeing a query first. Secondly, despite an initial positive response from an editor to a query, after seeing the manuscript the editor may reject it. In that case I

140

retype the front page and mail it out to the next name on my list. This saves time and mental energy as I do not have to go through the decision process again for that particular article. By working my way down the list, rejection is never considered to be final until all possible leads have been exhausted.

Rejected manuscripts are then placed into a file marked "Rejected" awaiting possible revision in the future if a new market comes to my attention or I learn of some newer information that might help sell the article. About a year ago I went through my rejected file. It contained some 40 pieces most of which had been written more than five years ago. Although the majority appeared outdated and I felt could not be resuscitated, I did manage to update several stories and sell them.

Despair and despondency are normal reactions for writers. I learned this from the responses received in answer to the questionnaire that I had sent some of my writing friends. Syndicated columnist Bette Elliott wrote that beginning writers tend to become discouraged or angry at rejections. Learn how to overcome these rejections by talking to selling authors, and submitting manuscripts in the correct form, she said.

Dina Donohue, contributing editor to *Guideposts*, urged that "a beginner, indeed any writer, should not be unduly discouraged by rejection slips. What is not suitable for one publication might be welcome elsewhere. Learn from criticism—rewrite and revise."

"You need to develop patience," said Ruth Moose, a highly successful free-lance writer. "Patience to revise and revise and revise again. Patience to keep trying a story in the markets, even the 27th time." In the section on Fiction, Moose tells about her persistence that has paid off in sales.

Conference consultant Doris Marston believes that the reason some beginners have trouble in selling their work is because they fail to do sufficient planning and investigation of the subject about which they are writing.

Martha Monigle, ghostwriter, teacher, and author, went into the matter of presentation in more detail when she said, "Since editors will not read past the first page if the script contains errors in spelling, punctuation and grammar, writers

need to study and review textbooks." Martha also passed on suggestions from her creative writing students on how to avoid rejection. They include:
* Reread work later and prune it
* Take time to mull over and not rush to mail out your manuscript.
* Get another person's viewpoint
* Revise after sending it out five times
* Read and analyze published works of others.

Rejection slips should never be regarded as a personal rejection of you as an individual. They may not even be criticisms of your work but merely inform you that the editor had no need for that material. In order to sell, your story has to fall into the right hands at the right moment. If the editor has just bought a similar piece your only recourse is to try another publication.

If an editor makes comments about your writing when turning it down it pays to study the comments because they may reveal why your story was rejected. It may not be an outright rejection, the editor may be offering you a second chance at submission if you follow the suggestions he or she has made. For example, the editor may write that the story needs "strengthening, tightening, or more detail." You may be asked to shorten or lengthen the story to meet the publication's requirements. If you feel these suggestions have merit, revise along the lines suggested and resubmit to that same market. You may be warmly received and the editor will certainly know that you are serious about trying to work with the publication.

If all you are getting are printed rejection slips in response to your submissions you might take a critical look to see whether you are sending your manuscripts to the right markets. I do believe there are plenty of markets looking for good material but it takes careful study to match your material to the market that wants it. Is your material of similar quality to other material published by this market? Is yours a familiar subject merely warmed over? Are you sure you've offered the reader something new on the topic? Has the market been glutted with similar stories on this same topic? If your story follows an overkill of the topic put it away for six months or a year and then resuscitate it by adding new material before sending it out again. Having had a respite from the topic the reading public may be interested to get an update.

Above all, don't let rejection slips stop you from working. Keep on writing and circulating your stories. Try the smaller magazines first, those that do not rely on staff-written material. Once you've been accepted by the smaller magazines you can then set your sights higher and aim for the larger circulation glossy magazines. Your growing list of published credits will be testimony to the confidence that other editors had in your writing and the confidence you have in your own ability. Rejection slips will no longer daunt you, because they will diminish in importance as your list of published works grows.

See also Selling Your Work

RESEARCH AND NOTE-TAKING

"Get your facts first, and then you can distort 'em
as you please." — Mark Twain

The ability to write a solid nonfiction article often depends
on the amount of research you carry out. Adequate research
includes advance reading, observation, and digging for facts,
sifting through the ideas and opinions of others, and gathering
information first-hand either by conducting personal or written interviews. Don't be surprised if you find yourself spending more time on researching than writing the story. Your
finished piece may include only a small fraction of the material you gathered originally but the exploration and consideration you put into the work will be reflected in the quality of
your writing.

Pete Ivey, who was for many years the Director of the
News Bureau of The University of North Carolina at Chapel
Hill, once said you must look for facts that are new and
known by few when you do your research. In Pete's own
words, taken from one of his lectures, here is how you should
get started with your research:

> Go on a hunting expedition. Read books, maga-
> zines, and newspapers. Find out what the authori-
> ties have said. Dig for facts until you have found
> that you have mastered the subject, at least
> adequately for your present purposes. Interview
> people who have information. Then investigate
> further until you have discovered some facts that
> are new and known by few.

The way a beginning writer gets started on research varies
greatly with the subject. Richard Cole, Dean of the School of
Journalism, University of North Carolina, told me at an interview, "There is a book way of doing research and the people
way. First of all you have to isolate your subject. Read and

find out all you can about it. Go to your library and ask your librarian for help. Use indexes, biographies, dictionaries, catalogs, in order to yield the information you want. Then you are ready to go on to the second stage of research—that is, you consult and obtain information from experts. On any college campus there are experts in virtually everything; go to them for further information."

What can you do if you are not near a college town? "Look for help from the federal and state government agencies," said Cole. "They are enormous fountains of information and you can conduct a lot of research by mail." Besides the government agencies and organizations there are national organizations, professional societies, business and special interest groups that are receptive to working with writers if you explain what it is you want from them.

Gaining quick and ready access to information is often simply a matter of knowing the right name and the right number to call. A most valuable reference work for information gatherers is Rod Norland's *Names and Numbers: A Journalist's Guide to the Most Needed Information Sources and Contacts.* This is a comprehensive directory with over 20,000 listings of information sources and contacts. It includes special interest groups, institutions, sports leagues and teams, political parties, labor unions, federal, state, regional, county and city government offices, scientific societies, public relations firms, and people in all walks of life. (Other reference sources will be found in the sections on Idea Origination and Use Your Public Library.)

Note-Taking

Be ready to take notes wherever you are. "Always have some sort of writing implement and paper with you, or be prepared to write on a tablecloth or napkin," says Cole. Alternatively, you might prefer using a tape recorder. They have become so commonplace that few people nowadays freeze up at the sight of them. Whether writing or recording find the system that works best for you and stick to it.

Go over your notes as quickly as possible after you've conducted an interview. This will give you the opportunity to accurately recall the details of setting, characteristics of the

145

interview, and show up any incomplete notes or omissions of importance. If you find some areas need elaboration or more explanation it is better to make a telephone call to the source as soon after the interview as you can.

Some writers get so carried away chasing new leads and collecting more and more data that they put off the assembly of the material and the writing of the story until they have acquired masses of information (sometimes far more than they need). Eventually, however, even the most ardent researcher must cease the gathering of new information and get down to the business of writing. That involves analyzing, rejecting, or including the information that has been gathered. As Barzun and Graff put it, "the facts never speak for themselves. They must be selected, marshalled, linked together, and given a voice. Obviously, research is not an end to itself. The day comes when the pleasures and the drudgery of the detective hunt are over and the report must be written."

One of the rewarding elements of writing is that in the process of selection, rejection, comparisons, and contrasts, you may find that you have uncovered some new idea. You have had an inspired thought and produced an original view of the subject. This new thought or new way of saying something is very satisfying to the writer because it is what will make a manuscript stand out from all others. Editors are constantly looking for something new, something different, something interesting. Originality is what they are after no matter what phrase they use.

After you've written your story what are you going to do with all those notes, clippings, letters and such? Do not throw them away! Keep them to refer to later, either for verification of your statements, should they ever be questioned by a doubting reader, or to use for another story. Dennis Hensley, a master at producing multiple stories from the same basic research, explains how to re-use material in his section on Multiple Sales of Articles.

See also Idea Origination
Multiple Sales of Articles
Use Your Public Library

REVISE AND REWRITE

"You become a good writer just as you become a
good joiner; by planing down your sentences."
— Antole France

Almost as much time should be spent on revising and
rewriting as you spend on thinking, planning, and putting
your writing into rough draft form. "Thinkee long; write
chop-chop," was the way Pete Ivey used to describe the task
of revising. Pete was News Bureau Director for the University
of North Carolina at Chapel Hill when he presented an excellent lecture on the subject of revision to the Tar Heel Writers
Roundtable in 1972. Revision or editing is not a restriction
on the creative spirit, he said. Quite the contrary, it is a
freedom to be enjoyed. Keep at it until you either run out of
time or can't bear the thought of reading your story even one
more time.

"Some great writers have dashed off gems the first time,
but usually even the greatest rewrite over and over and over.
It's fun to rub out words you have written and substitute
words that have clarity and give sharper meaning to what you
have first written. You may find you've used the same verb
too often, if so, find another verb. The second one will
probably be better," said Ivey.

"Re-think your ideas until they are clear. Don't try to say
too many things at once. If a sentence sounds awkward on
re-reading what you have written, rephrase the sentence. Chop
a long sentence in two, cauterize the wound and capitalize the
first word in the second sentence and you have it made. You
give the reader two simple sentences instead of one that is
long, compound, or complex."

When you are revising, you should have close at hand a
book of synonyms and antonyms and a dictionary. Synonyms
are words that are similar in meaning, antonyms are words
that are opposite. For example, if you look up the word

147

"fiction" you will learn the synonyms are: myth, fable, story, or creation; whereas the antonyms are: history, fact, reality, truth. Consult any of the following books when you want to freshen and enlarge your word vocabulary.

Dictionaries of Synonyms and Antonyms
> Roget, Peter Mark. *New Roget's Thesaurus of the English Language in Dictionary Form.* Revised edition by Norman Lewis. P. Putnam's Sons, NY. 1965.
> *Webster's Dictionary of Synonyms.* G. & C. Merriam, Springfield, MA. 1968.
> *Webster's Collegiate Thesaurus.* G. & C. Merriam, Springfield, MA. 1978.

How to Revise and Rewrite
"Write in haste, revise at leisure," was another of Ivey's proverbs with punch. It is easier to revise if you allow some time to elapse between the first and second draft. Areas that need reworking seem to leap off the page if I wait for a couple of days before re-reading my first draft. If you can't take an overnight break, read the story aloud or have someone read it to you. Better still, tape it, then listen to your own voice reading the copy. It is amazing how oral presentation will uncover writing weaknesses.

I make my first draft revisions with a pair of scissors and a pen, slicing apart paragraphs and inserting them in a better location. I may add new thoughts or delete some material at this stage. This "cut-and-paste" copy is then retyped as a second draft. The next stage is to take this clean copy and give it a careful reading, adding transitions to link the paragraphs, and reworking the material so that it flows even better than before.

Depending upon the extent of my revisions to the second draft, I may retype the whole article again. At this stage the retyping may include further word changes or repositioning. I then give it a final reading for grammar and spelling and am then ready to go ahead with typing the final form of the manuscript.

The number of revisions is entirely up to the writer. Some writers say they can produce final copy after only one or two revisions. Others will tell you they may rework parts of a chapter seven to ten times before they are satisfied with the results. It is important to know when to stop revising. Be assured that it is the rare piece that appears perfect to the writer. Yet, at some point one must stop if only because of lack of time. When revising your work watch out that you don't sacrifice a happy spontaneity in favor of a tired correctness.

See Manuscript Preparation and Mailing

RIGHTS FOR SALE

When you create a piece of writing you own all rights to that work. It is yours to sell or give away, to use in any form you wish written or oral. The most significant proposition of the 1978 Copyright Law is that editors and publishers now have to obtain rights in writing, or they don't have them. Unless you sign an agreement to the contrary you own what you create. You can make more money by refusing to assign all rights to the first purchaser. By holding on to subsidiary rights you are free to sell your story or article to more than one market. Dennis Hensley describes this in detail in his section on Multiple Sales of Articles.

Be careful where you permit your writing to be published. You may lose your copyright if your work appears in an uncopyrighted newspaper or magazine without your copyright notice on it. Therefore, your first step towards protecting your work should be to place your copyright announcement ((c) your name followed by the date) on the first page of every manuscript you send out. This indicates to everyone that it is your own work and they may not use it without your permission. Although the copyright notice does not take the place of a formal application to the Copyright Office, it is a method of announcing to everyone that you have owner-ship. Copyright registration, on the other hand, is a formal legal notification that may be used in a court of law.

State the Rights You Are Selling

It is best to state which rights you are selling when you offer your work to an editor or publisher, so that you can withdraw your offer before publication if you feel the pay-ment they discuss is insufficient. In the top right-hand corner of the first page of each manuscript, immediately below my copyright notice, I type the rights I am offering, like this:

(c) Rita Berman July 1980
First North American Rights.

150

Rights Can Be Divided Into Many Categories

Avoid selling "all rights" to your work. If you sell all rights you relinquish the right to reap further monetary gains from that work and the buyer can sell it to others or use it over and over again without paying you one cent more. You no longer have the right to use that particular piece in its present form. You may use some of the ideas expressed but they have to be rephrased and changed substantially so as not to appear to be the same story.

Try to negotiate with the purchaser so that you sell "first rights only." This will allow the buyer to be the first user, one time only, and within a certain period. Unless he uses the material within a year the rights revert back to you. After the buyer of the first rights has used the material, you are free to resell it for second rights, reprint rights, and so on.

"First serial rights" is the description you would use when offering the right to use your story in a periodical publication. When you sell first serial rights you still own, among other things, first book rights. After the story has appeared in the magazine, you are free to sell second serial rights to another periodical, and so on down the line just as long as you find publications who are willing to buy. (See Dennis Hensley's description of this ripple-effect in his section on Multiple Sales.)

Remember the Foreign Markets

If you sell your story for "First North American serial rights only," you retain the option to sell the identical story to foreign markets. (First North American serial rights means you are offering the right to use your material for the first time in any periodical in North America.) If the purchaser accepts these terms, then, even before it gets published, you are free to locate markets abroad and sell them the rights to publish the story in their country. You may even sell first United Kingdom rights to a periodical in England, for instance, and then offer the First North American rights to a market at home.

Reprint rights are another means of producing later sales with very little effort. The *Reader's Digest* is one market that frequently reprints selections from other magazines. If you've sold all rights to the other publication, however, you won't get one cent of the reprint rights fee paid by *Reader's Digest* unless you have had the rights reassigned back or there has been an agreement in writing about sharing the income from reprint rights.

How can you prevent signing away more rights than you want to sell? This question comes up because of the practice employed by some publishers of stamping the terms and conditions on the back of their payment check. If you endorse the check, have you signed an agreement and thus signed away more rights than you wanted to sell? Some writers advise that all you need to do is deposit the check unsigned into your bank account. If the check is made out to the same name as on your bank account then the bank will automatically credit it to your account, so they say. I think the first thing you might do is talk to your bank manager before you deposit the check to make sure that not signing it presents no problem. Even better, because this is a question relating to contract law which varies from state to state, get your lawyer's opinion on how to handle this situation.

Can your work be used without your permission? It shouldn't be, but sometimes it happens that your writing is republished without your prior agreement. The worst thing is, you may never find out.

Here's an experience that I had a couple of years ago. I sold first rights for a feature, was paid on acceptance, the feature subsequently was published, and I received a file copy from the magazine. About a year later a friend told me that he had read my feature in a magazine he had picked up in his doctor's office. I had no record of selling my story to that magazine. I was mystified and slightly annoyed at the thought that my story had been used and I had not profited by it. I wrote to the purchaser of the first rights and asked if they were the publishers of the magazine in which my story had been reprinted. In my letter I mentioned that I had sold only first rights to the story and so whomever had used it for the second time owed me money. I asked if they could shed any light on the matter.

Back came an apologetic letter saying they had indeed used my story for a second time, in one of their other publications, but they didn't realize at the time that they had to pay for it. The error occurred, said the editor, because their usual practice was to buy all rights. However, on checking they discovered my manuscript had the words "First North American rights only" typed on it. I received a check for the reprint rights some 30 days later, but I was left with an uneasy feeling. How many of my articles have been reprinted in obscure magazines without my knowledge? Even if I had sold all rights to a story I'd certainly be interested to know if it was used several times and where. At the very least I could add the names of the publications to my list of credits.

In the case of a sale made to an uncopyrighted publication and if the material does not carry your copyright notice, you would have no recourse against anyone using that material. Most newspapers and some magazines are not copyrighted. Should your work appear in these publications without a copyright notice it could fall into the public domain. The result is some loss of copyright protection and, unless corrected within five years, in the complete loss of copyright. Copyright protection cannot be restored for any work that has already gone into the public domain.

When selling to uncopyrighted publications, this is how you should protect your material. Arrange, in advance, and on acceptance of the manuscript, that your copyright symbol, the date, and your name will appear on the first page of the article, story, or poem in the magazine. This costs the magazine nothing. You pay to register the copyright. On publication, send two copies of the page or pages on which your story appears, to the Register of Copyrights, with a check for $10 and a completed application form appropriate for a "Contribution to a Periodical." Further information about the procedure for correcting errors or omissions may be obtained by writing to the Copyright Office, Library of Congress, Washington, D.C. 20559.

See also Copyright Law and Registration Procedures
Legal Information for the Writer
Multiple Sales of Articles

SELLING YOUR WRITING

"Half my lifetime I have earned my living by selling words, and I hope thoughts."

— Winston Churchill

The beginning writer may ask the question, "Where can I sell it?" after writing a feature story. The professional non-fiction writer, however, already experienced in writing and selling will frequently not write a word until the marketing question has been answered. Actually, the beginner who asks about "selling" is on the right track even if his timing is off. Far too many writers just give their work away; for them the gratification of seeing their words in print is sufficient payment. "Don't give your work away. If it's worth publishing it's worth paying for," said one writer.

Although only a small number of writers are able to make a living by free-lance writing, there are thousands who reap pleasure from receiving checks that cover their postage bill for the month, buy the groceries, or help pay the rent. Where you sell depends on what you write. Consumer magazines will buy articles, informal essays, short stories, poetry, and fillers. Trade and business journals need business interviews, reports of new story openings, business methods, and product information. Special interest magazines want stories that are very individualized and cater to a particular group of people.

Certain types of writing sell better than others. For instance, it's easier to sell a magazine article than a short story these days. With over 22,000 publications using articles there are abundant opportunities for a writer to find an outlet for creative work. Some writers say you should start at the top and work down. I disagree with this sales philosophy. I'll let Curtis Casewit, author of *Freelance Writing* explain why:

The magazine world can be compared to a pyramid. The mass markets stand on a tiny summit platform. They're almost unreachable. . .fees for writers can run from $1,500 to $5,000. . . .A handful of literary agents and a stable of old-timers do most of the selling here. . . .

Casewit is of the opinion, and I agree with him, that only rarely do novices have the contacts or the needed writing polish to crash these markets. Continuing with his market description, Casewit notes:

> The prestige markets form the next-to-top level of the pyramid. Their circulation is small, and pay rates fluctuate between $200 and $800 an article. These publications are equally difficult to hit unless you're an authority. The newcomer is not unwelcome, but a first article rarely has enough depth or style for the sophisticated magazines.

For the part-time writer, the widest and most accessible section of the pyramid are the secondary magazines. Here's where you can make sales! These magazines may not always be found on the newsstands, many are available by subscription only. But they have a need for steady, reliable writers and they are willing to read a beginner's work. Such periodicals may deal with a single topic, such as surfing, boating, or camping, or be aimed at a special group, such as political, fraternal, ethnic, or religious.

The Markets and Pay Scales
There are more than 50 categories of consumer publications and at least 80 categories of business, trade, technical, and professional journals listed in *The Writer's Market*. When I analyzed the various categories of consumer publications I found that pay scales ranged from one cent to one dollar and more a word. Certain categories pay more than others, as will be seen from this list:

155

Category of Consumer Publication	Pay Range	Rate, Per Word
Animals and pets	medium	2 - 10 cents
Art	low	1 - 5
Astrology	low	2 - 6
Automobile	high	5 - 50
Confessions	low	3 - 5
Food and drink	medium	2 - 8
Health	medium	2 - 10
Hobby and craft	low	1 - 10
Home and garden	high	10 - $1
Juvenile	low	2 - 5
Literary	poor	1 cents and up
Men's Interest	high	1 - 30
Music	low	1 - 5
Regional	medium	1 - 10
Sports	high	5 - 30
Theatre	low	1 - 20
Women's Interest	high	20 - $1 and up

Pay scales for the business, trade, technical, and professional journals varied from two to 15 cents and more a word.

Selling Your Writing

How much money can you make from writing? What do these rates mean in terms of your effort and out-of-pocket expenses? Is one cent a word "making money?" Is ten cents? A dollar? At what pay can a free-lance writer make money. One cent a word is a ridiculous amount. It takes me an hour of preparation, research, interviewing, and writing to produce 100 words for my business stories. If I accepted one cent a word for my writing output I'd only be earning one dollar an hour. Increase the rate to five cents a word and I would still make more typing someone else's manuscript. Most of the markets that I work for pay from ten to fifteen cents a word. I regret to report that I've seen very little evidence of magazine publishers raising their rates in order to help the free-lance writer offset the increased costs of paper, postage, and

156

other business expenses. According to market reports, some magazines are attempting to solve their money problems in these inflationary times by switching to payment on publication instead of on acceptance. This makes the situation worse not better for their writers.

No matter what rate you are getting, if you are only making infrequent sales, then take a look at what you are writing and the audience you want to reach. Are you restricting your sales because there are too few markets for the material you are writing? The ease with which you can make a sale depends, to a large extent, on the type of story you have written. A feature with universal appeal could be placed with any general interest magazine, whereas a story covering an obscure or specialized subject will naturally be more difficult to sell.

Advice From the Professionals On How to Sell

The following comments are representative of the replies I received to my questionnaire. They relate to the question: "Where do beginning writers have the most trouble in selling their work?"

Martha Monigle wrote: "Many writers have trouble in selling because they aim for the wrong markets or don't know how to analyze the markets."

"Writers must know their editor's requirements. Never send out material unless you have read the magazine, newspaper, or similar books by the selected publisher," said Doris Marston.

"Find one place to sell and go from there," suggested Cookie McGee.

"Start small (local papers, magazines). Remember, nonfiction outsells fiction. Poetry does not sell much unless one is famous," said Bette Elliott.

If you are working on a book, you can sell chapters as articles, reserving book rights for later use, advised Dina Donohue, contributing editor of *Guideposts*.

Dennis Hensley replied: "Beginning writers usually work like crazy on one article idea and then, after it sells, they move to another project without remarketing the original article several more times." The way to remarket your material, said Hensley, is to hold the copyright ownership of

157

everything you produce. Sell from the smallest markets towards the biggest markets (from local papers to state papers to national magazines.)

Broaden your writing interests and you will find it easier to make sales. When you write for a wide range of publications you increase your opportunities for sales and resales. Follow Hensley's advice and send your manuscripts to non-overlapping markets. In this way you produce multiple sales from one story.

Be persistent. Do not let your selling efforts flag if some of your articles are returned unsold. Send them out again and again. Retype the manuscript if it appears soiled or dog-eared. If you have already prepared a list of possible markets, as I suggested in the section on How To Avoid Rejection, it will lessen your feelings of disappointment and enable you to put the manuscript back into circulation with a minimum of delay.

See also Market Listings
Rejections—Avoiding Them
Rights for Sale

STYLE

Writing is a very personal activity that reflects the uniqueness of the writer. Even if ten different writers used the same outline and reference material they would interpret the facts differently and produce ten different articles. This difference is called style and can be the hallmark of a writer. Style also varies from writer to writer according to the kind of material being created.

In nonfiction writing, communication is the primary purpose, therefore clarity is more important than an original or complex style. The writing must be clear, direct in presentation of facts, and easy to read. Select specific and concrete words that tell your story simply. Avoid cliches, hackneyed phrases, and abstract generalities.

Fiction writing permits greater flexibility of style, for the plot, characters, and dramatic setting spring from the author's imagination. Here the writer is encouraged to use colorful, bright language to create a mood and sustain the reader's interest.

Despite their differences, both fields of writing call for attention to grammar, syntax, punctuation, and spelling. By following the "20 Rules For Good Writing," set down by the Writer's Digest School, and reprinted below by permission, you should produce the type of writing that most editors buy:

1. Prefer the plain word to the fancy.
2. Prefer the familiar word to the unfamiliar.
3. Prefer the Saxon word to the Romance.
4. Prefer nouns and verbs to adjectives and adverbs.
5. Prefer picture nouns and action verbs.
6. Never use a long word when a short one will do as well.
7. Master the simple declarative sentence.
8. Prefer the simple sentence to the complicated.
9. Vary your sentence length.

10. Put the words you want to emphasize at the beginning or end of your sentence.
11. Use the active voice.
12. Put statements in a positive form.
13. Use short paragraphs.
14. Cut needless words, sentences, and paragraphs.
15. Use plain, conversational language. Write like you talk.
16. Avoid imitation. Write in your natural style.
17. Write clearly.
18. Avoid gobbledygook and jargon.
19. Write to be understood not to impress.
20. Revise and rewrite. Improvement is always possible.

See also Grammar and Spelling
Revise and Rewrite
Writing Tips

SYNDICATING
(c) 1980 by Bette Elliott

(This section has been contributed by Bette Elliott. Ms. Elliott has been self-syndicating her newspaper column, The Handicapped Mailbag, for the past two years. Her feature articles have appeared in numerous state and national magazines for North Carolina newspapers. She is the author of *The Clockwatchers' Cookbook* (Moore Publishing Co.) and is now working on a novel. She is managing editor of the Bill Kiser News Service of Raleigh.)

Travel writer Kay Cassill calls the malady "Syndicatus Syndromis." I call it madness. But who am I to dissuade any beginner from going after the big bucks and bigger reader count than any writer of novels, nonfiction or poetry could ever dream of?

The syndication route is a brutal one and is only for the brave and foolhardy and tough-skinned. If you are currently writing a column for your local newspaper and have developed a fine rapport with your readers who, judging from your mail, think your work is fantastic, you could try to increase your readership (and income) by self-syndicating it. If your editor likes your work and you, he may suggest that a national syndicate would be interested in taking a look at it. The editor has many contacts in the syndicating world (after all, he's besieged every day by salesmen who want to sell him columns, features, comic strips, and puzzles that are guaranteed to double his circulation in two weeks), so through his contacts, your editor could send off samples of your work and a glowing letter about your sparkling wit and ability to crank out first class stuff year after year.

What are your chances of success, whether you self-syndicate or get your influential editor to persuade a syndicate to handle you? I don't like to dampen your spirits by saying "a million to one," but I will say that you might enjoy a modest fame if you self-syndicate your work in your

161

home state. As for a national syndicate snapping up your efforts, you must remember these truths:

* Until Erma Bombeck goes her great reward, funny house-
    wives can save their strength and write about
    something else.
* Abby and Ann have cornered the lovelorn market (and
    increasingly are getting into the mental health and
    consumer field), so if your column is advice-oriented,
    forget that, too.
* Political pundits must be Washington-based to be nation-
    ally syndicated.
* Your wonderful "down-home" philosophy will rate a
    crashing zero with sophisticated urban readers.
* Gardening? Fine for your own area, but what do you
    know about soil conditions in Arizona?

What I'm getting at is this: There are only so many column categories that national syndicates will even consider, and professionals of long standing have cornered the market pretty well. Columns fall into specific categories:

Opinion Columns

These are written by veteran political analysts and commentators like James Reston and William Buckley.

Essay Columns

The authors hook their readers as much with their felicity of prose as they do with what they have to say. Many have already distinguished themselves with novels or as lecturers. Humor is the most obvious mode here (Russell Baker, Art Buchwald are exponents of this genre as is the afore-mentioned Mrs. Bombeck), and then there are the urban "poets" like Jimmy Breslin and the late Neyer Berger. Sydney Harris, with his highly personal brand of philosophy, is another writer in this category.

Leisure and Entertainment

These are the syndicated astrologers, bridge masters, television writers, authorities (always renowned) on house plants, pop music and so on.

Advice

To the love lorn, to the consumer, to the single, to the senior citizen, to the health nut, to the small investor. The writers are all professionals (although the Dear Abby/Ann Landers success stories, widely publicized, are exceptions. The twins happened to have good luck and editors who loved them).

Fillers

These are the Laugh-a-Day, clever couplets, prayers, word games, odd facts and so on that all newspapers carry (and which, if Divine Providence would have it, offer an excellent starter for the would-be syndicated writer, if he or she has an idea that has not been used before).

If your column doesn't fit in any of the above categories, don't despair. You must believe in your work, know that your idea is unique, and your local readership is strong. Then you can think about self-syndicating. During your plans for expanding your work, keep this in mind: most syndicated columnists didn't enjoy overnight fame. Most of them started with a local paper, worked very, very, very hard, collected some of their best columns and printed a modest book, went on the local lecture and talk show circuit, became big local celebrities, and finally after a dozen years of this, saw their work "take off" as they say in syndication land.

Self-syndication is a business and you must be businesslike in your approach to it. Ask yourself these questions:

Am I a disciplined person?

Can I take a flat "no" from my prospective customers without crawling in a corner with hurt feelings?

Am I able to outline and follow through with a selling campaign?

How much should I charge for my column?

Am I able to keep books, maintain clean neat files, and records of expenses for travel and printing and mailing?

Will I suffer if an editor accepts my column and then cancels after a few weeks trial?

If you can "psych" yourself into a businesslike frame of mind and realize that not every editor is going to think your

163

column is marvelous (Some won't even see you. They don't like to spend money on anything.), that selling is the roughest business in the world for sensitive types, and that you may not make a single sale, then go ahead with your campaign. Faint heart never syndicated a column.

Your first step is to lay out a bit of money on a brochure that tells prospective customers all about your column and you. It should have a picture of you on the front, surrounded by snippets of praise from your most prominent readers and friends, people whose names would be instantly recognized. Your brochure should, in glowing terms, tell why the inclusion of your column in a newspaper will bring that enterprise untold riches and enormous readership. It should contain a "rate card." This means the amount of money you are charging each paper according to the paper's circulation.

What should you charge? This is a question only you can answer. Your editor might tell you what he pays for work similar to yours, but as a beginner you can't expect to be rewarded as handsomely as the Nation's Funniest Housewife. I can only advise and if you disagree, that's okay. You are the person who sets the value on your work, not me. A beginner, selling in his or her home state, would be smart not to charge more than $2 or $2.50 per column for weeklies and papers under 20,000 circulation; more than $5 per column for papers, 20,000-50,000; more than $7.50 for papers 50,000-100,000; and $10 per column for papers over that number.

Oh, I know. It's a pittance. But you want to sell your work, don't you? These days, editors are extremely cautious, money-wise. They'll give you every excuse under heaven for not buying ("we don't have the space. . ." ". . .we're cutting back and not adding new features. . ." "your column is fine but I can't see that it has any readership," and so on). Your come-back is your mail pull, your vast local readership, your marvelous personality, and your low price. Especially your low price.

Some editors you hope to convince of your special talents will ask if they can "try out" your column for a few weeks (gratis) to see if it has the magic potential you claim for it. Do not do this. Tell the rascal your policy is not to give away your work because your expenses do not cover such a gift and you are terribly sorry but your column is $2.50 (or $5, $7.50 or $10 depending on circulation) even during a trial period. The editor will respect your business acumen (he never gave anything away, either), and may very well become your best customer.

When you self-syndicate your work, you must have a legal agreement. A lawyer will draw one up for you for about $50 (or your home town editor could get the newspaper's lawyer to do it for you). The agreement simply states that you will provide your customer with X number of columns per week, that you will mail the columns in time for certain agreed-upon deadlines, and that the paper will pay you X number of dollars per column. The agreement should also state that the paper has the privilege of cancelling the column by giving you, the author, two weeks notice.

Here are some helpful hints for your selling success: Write a once-a-week column at first. Most editors are not interested in daily columns or even twice-a-week columns for economic reasons.

Deal only with the person on the paper's staff who has the power to buy your work. Every newspaper has a different pecking order. Sometimes the managing editor is more powerful than the editor. Sometimes the feature editor is more powerful than anybody. It is a very strange situation, and you have to do some careful checking before you approach a newspaper. I have found that the publisher is the person to write to and that worthy will see to it that the proper person receives your proposal. This holds true, however, only if the publisher is actively involved in the day-to-day operation of the paper. (Many newspapers today are owned by out-of-state moguls. Check! And double check! You must be extremely cautious and approach the right person.)

After you have sent your letter and brochure to the right person, follow this mailer with a telephone call and make an appointment to see the right person. Then keep the appointment. And be on time. You should take with you samples of your best work, your biography and your agreement—and a positive attitude. If you are so lucky as to make a sale, write your customer a thank-you note immediately upon your return to home base.

As soon as you have signed up even one paper, you are a syndicated writer and you should begin sending out your column. Pace yourself, however. Don't try to sell every paper in the state in the first two weeks. Keep in mind, too, that you will, if you are a good salesman, average one "Yes" sale to every three "No" sales. Don't let the "No" sales discourage you. Have faith in what you are doing, and keep on trying. You might pay a friendly call to a "No sale" six months after the turn-down and find a new editor sitting there who loves the sight of you and thinks your column is marvelous and buys it on the spot. In this business, you never can tell when luck will be on your side.

After selling and promoting your column for a few years, you may want to "go national" as they say. Again, your brochure, your successes, and your testimonials get to work for you. Mail your package out to the top syndicate in the land, and wait. And wait. And wait some more. But what is this? A letter? From ABC Syndicate? To you? With a contract? Offering you 50 percent of the profits? A sales force at-the-ready to place your scintillating column in 400 newspapers throughout the land? Book suggestions? Clarion calls to appear on the big TV talk shows? To be the speaker at national conventions? With potential earnings of $500,000 a year, and a readership of vast millions? Maybe. Anyone can dream. Why not you?

The top syndicates, the people who could make that dream come true because they have the money to promote your work and the sales force to sell it, are these:

Chicago Tribune-New York News Syndicate
220 East 42nd Street, New York NY 10017

Field Newspaper Syndicate
401 N. Wabash Avenue, Chicago, IL 60611

King Features Syndicate
235 E. 45th Street, New York, NY 10017

Newspaper Enterprise Association
200 Park Avenue, New York, NY 10017

166

United Feature Syndicate
200 Park Avenue, New York, NY 10017

Columbia Features, Inc.
36 W. 44th Street, New York, NY 10036

The Register and Tribune Syndicate
715 Locust Street, Des Moines, IA 50304

I have not included the names of editors with this list as they change with the wind. You must check, first, to make certain your mailer reaches the right person.

Publications you might find helpful include: A roster of all newspapers in the state including circulation figures as well as the names of the top brass, put out by your state's press association; *The Writer's Market* offers listings of all syndicates, large and small, their current needs, and suggestions for beginners. This book is published annually and is available in all well-stocked bookstores; The annual *Editor and Publisher*, magazine's list of syndicated columns. Your editor no doubt subscribes to this publication. Your local library will have a copy of it.

Good luck!

TITLES TALK

Titles are not tags to be tacked onto your stories as an afterthought. They are the bait you use to attract editors and readers. A catchy, clever title can carry more weight than the lead paragraph. When creating titles avoid tongue-twisters or combinations of words that do not flow. Keep it short. Most magazine titles rarely exceed six to eight words; although substitutes may run a little longer. A good title should be indicative of the contents and tone of the story. Some writers wait until they complete the story before creating its title, although they may use a working title until a better one comes to mind. Titles cannot be copyrighted.

Titles can be grouped into categories, as shown below. All of the examples given have been published.

Alliterative: Repetition of initial letters or sounds to produce a melodious title.
"From Horseback to Helicopter." — Rita Berman
"Pumping the Profs." — Dennis Hensley
"The Whys of Working Wives." — Marjorie Holmes

Controversial: Debatable statement. Produces a "show-me" reaction in reader.
"Reston, Virginia: Life in a Goldfish Bowl." — Rita Berman

Dramatic: Plays upon the feelings rather than logic.
"Growing Older Affects Us All." — Rita Berman
"The Saturday Evening Post Every Sunday Morning." — Ruth Moose

First Person: Experiences related by an individual.
"My Fifty Years in Golf." — Bob Hope
"We Sold Our Home." — Rita Berman

How-To: These tell the reader you are going to pass on some inside information or expertise.

168

"How To Win Friends and Influence People." — Dale Carnegie

"How To Train Workers." — Rita Berman

"How To Keep a Customer Cool." — Rita Berman

Label: Most effective on profiles or for summary and survey articles.

"Late Blooming Hoosier Actor Faces Busy Season." — Dennis Hensley

"The New Woman." — Rita Berman

Negative Headline: The appeal of the negative title is that words like "Not," "Never," and "Don't" have a shock value. In a title they serve as a red traffic light jarring the reader but grabbing his attention.

"Don't Poison Your Pet." — Rita Berman

"Men — Don't Be Ashamed To Cry." — Mort Weisinger

Number: Tells the reader how many points are covered or how much something costs, or how many people were involved.

"A Biography in Seven Lives." — Ruth Moose

"Three Ways to Cut Heating Bills." — Rita Berman

"The $2,000 Cooking Class." — Bruce David Colen

Phrase or Sentence: This may be a bit of dialogue taken directly from the article or it may be a single sentence. Effective in nostalgia or personal essay pieces.

"The A3 Doesn't Go to Portsmouth." — Rita Berman

"All Doors Led to the Kitchen." — Marjorie Holmes

"The Angel of the Lord and the One-Eyed Cow." — Ruth Moose

Question: The title challenges the reader to read the article and find out how the question is answered.

"Can Husbands and Wives Be Friends?" — Marjorie Holmes

"Can You Cash a $10,000 Bill?" — Mort Weisinger

"Should You Fight a Traffic Ticket?" — Mort Weisinger

Straight Advice or Statement: The implied message is "do it this way."

　　"Pick On the Shell Game." — Rita Berman

　　"What To Call a Mother-in-Law." — Martha Monigle

Superlative: About an individual who is unexcelled in some skill or performs an unsurpassed feat.

　　"Meet the Highest I.Q. In America." — Mort Weisinger.

See also Leads

TYPING TIPS

Typing your own manuscripts is an asset because you won't have to spend money on paying for a professional typist to prepare manuscripts that are as yet unsold. Hand-written submissions are not acceptable to editors. They are a dead giveaway that the writer is not a professional free-lancer. However, if you can't type well or don't have access to a machine, you have no alternative but to get outside help. Professional typists charge from 55 cents to $1 per double-spaced page plus postage, according to the advertisements in *Authorship* and *The Writer's Digest*. Check your local newspapers to see if the rates in your area are cheaper. Inquiries about typing charges in my area produced quotes that ranged from $1 to $2 per double-spaced page. I believe these higher rates are a result of the demand for typing services provided by the proximity of three universities in the area. Where there is less demand you would expect to pay a reasonable rate of no more than $1 per page.

Visually, there is a difference between manuscripts that are typed by a professional typist and those that are typed by someone who is unaware of the importance of framing words on paper. Faced with a slush pile of manuscripts, what editor could resist the appeal of a clean, error-free, neatly-typed manuscript. Such a manuscript inspires confidence that the author knows what he or she is doing. By contrast, a coffee-stained, dog-eared unevenly spaced manuscript that has been typed on thin, 9 lb paper is not going to evoke much enthusiasm from the editor.

Use Ample Margins

Typed copy, whether it is a letter or a page of manuscript, should appear to be framed by the white space. This calls for ample width margins at the top, bottom, and sides. Always leave sufficient margin on the left-hand side to permit the page to be hole-punched without encroaching upon the typed copy.

171

I type my manuscripts on an IBM Selectric$^{(R)}$ typewriter that has elite size type or 12 spaces to the horizontal inch. By setting my left-hand margin at 15 and the right-hand margin at 85 on the margin scale I get a 70-character line, approximately ten words per line. On a standard 8-1/2 x 11 inch page, I can type 250 words or 25 double-spaced lines of ten words each. A manuscript of 1500 words runs to six pages of elite type. If you are using a pica-size type (10 spaces per horizontal inch) you will get fewer words on the page.

Make A Typing Frame

Let me pass on to you an excellent tip I picked up at secretarial college more than thirty years ago. It will help you to frame your words with white space. First take a blank sheet of standard size typing paper (8-1/2 x 11 inches). Next, beginning one inch down from the top of the page, indent 1-1/2 inches and mark off a left-hand margin with a wide marking pen. Use a bright but strong color such as red. Then mark off the right-hand margin one inch from the edge of the right-hand side. Both margins should end one inch from the bottom of the page. Now connect up the lines from left to right at the top and bottom of the page. You should be left with a box measuring 6 x 9 inches within which to type your copy. Underline the place where title headings, your name, and the page number should go. If you follow this guide your manuscript will look uniform, page after page, and you will not have to worry about setting tabulation stops.

To use the frame, place your typing paper immediately over the marked-off page. The markings should be visible through the top sheet. Use a thicker pen or darker color if they are not. By using this frame you can avoid unnecessary retyping because you can see when you are getting close to the last line of typing on the page. When the bottom line of the frame shows underneath the top sheet, that should be your last line of typing. If by typing on that line you will be left with a one line carry over in the paragraph, then do not type on the bottom line. Instead, begin the next page with the last two lines of the paragraph.

Typing Business Letters

If you want to appear professional, then do observe standard business practice when sending out query letters and other business correspondence. Most letters are made up of the following components:

1. Letterhead or heading
2. Date
3. Name and address of the person to whom it is being sent
4. Salutation
5. Body of the letter
6. Complimentary close
7. Name of writer (typewritten)
8. Enclosure notification (if any sent).

Margins should be at least one inch on each side and one and a half inches at the bottom of the sheet. Most business letters are typed single-spaced with two spaces between paragraphs. Letters may be typed in either block or indented fashion. In the full block style the date, inside address, salutation, and all paragraphs begin flush with the left-hand margin.

With the indented form the first line of each paragraph is indented five spaces. The date may be centered or placed on the right-hand side of the paper. Two spaces below the date, type the name and address of the firm or person to whom you are writing. This section should be lined up with the left-hand margin. The salutation is written flush left and two spaces below the inside address. The complimentary close and signature are centered on the page.

Correct forms of salutation for business letters are:

1. Dear Sir:
2. Dear Mr. Smith:
3. Dear Mrs. Smith:
4. Gentlemen:
5. Ladies:
6. Ladies and Gentlemen:

A problem arises when the sex of the addressee is unknown, or when writing to an organization or group that may include women. For many people, the term "Gentlemen" is no longer acceptable. In cases like this, a male friend of mine addresses his letters "Dear Friends," and thus avoids being regarded as a sexist. Despite the seemingly casual tone I have on occasion followed his example.

Note that for business letters a colon (:) is used after the salutation but in personal correspondence the comma (,) is permitted.

The complimentary close, which ends with a comma, should be typed near the center of the page in the indented style, but flush left in the block style.

Some commonly used closings are:

1. Very truly yours,
2. Cordially yours,
3. Yours sincerely,
4. Sincerely,

The name of the sender should be typed at least four spaces below the closing words, leaving sufficient space for the signature. Postscripts are sometimes added to mention a forgotten item or to add emphasis to a point.

If the letter requires more than one page use a plain sheet of paper for the second sheet. Never type the continuation of a business letter on the reverse side of the sheet. On the second sheet at the left-hand margin type the name of the individual to whom you are writing. In the center type the page number and put the date so that it ends flush with the right-hand margin.

Always make a copy of your letters and manuscripts for your files. Standard copysets are available at your local stationery supply store, or you may simply insert a sheet of carbon paper between your stationery and the file copy. For the file copy use onionskin or low quality bond paper.

Typing addresses on envelopes

Commence the first line of the address slightly below the center of the envelope. If an address contains three lines or less, it may be double-spaced, although one sees this less frequently now.

Insert the letter into the envelope so that when the letter is removed and unfolded the typed side will face the reader.

To fold an 8-1/2 x 11 inch sheet to fit a No. 10 envelope (9-1/2 x 4-1/8 inches) fold from the top down. Make the fold about one third the length of the sheet. Next fold up from the bottom, leaving a half-inch margin at the first fold. When the letter is slipped into the envelope, the second fold is inserted towards the bottom of the envelope so that the half-inch margin ends up near the envelope flap. This makes it easy for the recipient to remove the letter and unfold it.

How To Improve Your Typing Speed

My advice for the way to improve your typing speed is the same as that for improving your writing skills. You must practice, practice, and practice some more. However, typing practice does not have to be a lot of boring work. Copy anything that is of interest to you. You might find it fun to try practicing the "fingerbenders" typing exercises suggested by the Smith-Corona Advisory Council (see below). They make an amusing change from the traditional sentence "quick brown fox jumps over the (lazy) dog's back."

Exercises

RAINDROPS KEEP FALLING ON MY HEAD whenever I try to pick LITTLE GREEN APPLES on RAINY DAYS and MONDAYS.   (20 words)

THE GREAT GATSBY was THE LAST TYCOON to make SUPERMONEY selling GREASE for HAIR.   (18 words)

ELEPHANTS CAN REMEMBER American Pie and Days of Future Passed, but Alice Cooper is too young to CATCH-22 or the NEW RIDERS OF THE PURPLE SAGE. (30 words)

BREAD and THE 5th DIMENSION are not in The FORSYTHE SAGA and neither are Jonathan Livingston Seagull and Kris Kristofferson.   (27 words)

SAD MOVIES ALWAYS MAKE ME CRY and THE LAST PICTURE SHOW was so sad, it had me standing in THE TRACKS OF MY TEARS.   (23 words)

175

To find out your correct words-per-minute speed, add up the number of words you typed and then deduct one word for each typing error from the total gross number. Divide the balance by the number of minutes spent in typing. The figure you arrive at is the number of words you type per minute.

To reduce fatigue when typing, keep your fingers well curved and strike with the ball of your fingers. Each hand should be anchored on the home keys with your little fingers serving as pivots. Keep your wrists down and "hug" the keyboard, roughly parallel with the slope of the keys, the Smith-Corona Advisory Council suggests. Maintain a continuous rhythm. Practice using your little finger to reach the carriage return key. It will save the bother of moving and returning your fingers to the home keys (asdf jkl;), while insuring continuous rhythm from one line to the next.

Further information on typing letters, minutes, reports, resumes and so on will be found in the following books:

Hutchinson, Lois I., *Standard Handbook for Secretaries*, McGraw-Hill, NY, 1972.

Skillin, Marjorie E., Robert M. Gay and other authorities, *Words Into Type*, Prentice-Hall, Inc., 3rd ed., NJ, 1974.

See also Manuscript Preparation and Mailing

USE YOUR PUBLIC LIBRARY

Your local public library is the place where you can find inspiration and information available absolutely free of charge. Use your librarian as a resource and you'll find digging for facts is not as complicated as you may have thought. Most librarians are enthusiastic about helping you search for articles and references, they will show and explain to you the card index used for cataloging books and how you can locate the material you need.

After you learn where the information is stored and how easy it is to retrieve, you'll be inclined to use your public library frequently as a stepping stone to further research. From published indexes and catalog you can learn what articles have been published on a particular topic, by whom, and when, and where the story appeared. With this information you will know if the ideas you are contemplating as feature stories have already been published. Through the numerous biographical indexes in the library you can locate more than one hundred thousand experts.

A good place to begin is with the card index file. This is a catalog of the author, and title, and topic of all books available on the library's shelves. Check the card file under the heading of the subject you intend to write about. Record the author and title of books to which you might refer. Also check the *Cumulative Book Index* which lists author, title, and subject of books published in English. *Books in Print* is another helpful annual catalog.

The Readers' Guide to Periodical Literature is helpful for locating what has already been published by the major magazines about a subject. In this you will find information that is too recent for books. Magazine articles are listed in the *Guide* by subject and by author's name and the date of publication. Other magazines, such as the secondary magazines or those with a specialized readership (*American Legion* magazine, *Weight Watchers'* magazine, etc.,) may be found in *Access* or *Abstracts of Popular Culture.*

177

The production of a well-rounded article requires more than a library search, it calls for people research. A lively quote from an expert will add sparkle to what might otherwise be a dull collection of facts. The task of tracking down the people to interview is simplified if you know where to find them. Sources that provide information on contemporary writers, scientists, lawyers and others are: *Current Biography*, published by H. H. Wilson Company and *Who's Who* volumes, published by Marquis. Many *Who's Who* volumes are divided according to region or profession, for example: *Who's Who in the South*, and *Who's Who in American Law*. These reference books list personal information about authorities and public figures, some of whom you may wish to contact for your story.

To make contact with these individuals it is best to write a brief letter stating your reasons for contacting them and the information you would like them to furnish. If they are too busy or too far away to be interviewed personally, submit your questions in the letter or offer your phone number and ask them to call you collect at some convenient time.

In addition to the general collection of books found at the public library there are also university libraries and special libraries not open to the general public. But many university and college libraries will open their reference shelves to the local townspeople and some even permit the borrowing of books. University libraries are the place to go for specialized indexes, such as *Education Index*, *Business Periodicals Index*, and *Psychological Abstracts*. Special libraries owned by private businesses and trade associations usually restrict their collections to one subject or a group of related subjects. Any library may allow you to use their books in the library if approached. The Head Librarian should be contacted for this permission, and will usually allow your use. If you live in a small town that has a limited library, write to your State library and find out how you may borrow books through inter-library loan.

See also Interviewing
Research and Note-taking

VOICE YOUR VIEWS

Expressing your views on a topic that is currently being discussed in your local community is an excellent way to break into print. A letter to the Editor of your local newspaper voicing your opinion of an issue or commenting on an article that has appeared recently in that paper has a good chance of being printed as long as you keep it brief and to the point. Most newspapers run a notice on the editorial page to the effect that letters are welcome but must be kept to a prescribed length. Your letter should attack issues, not people, and must be free of expletives. It should also be signed and contain your address. Some newspapers restrict the letters they will publish from the same person to only one a month.

The personal essay is another method of voicing your views. These essays are usually published in literary magazines, but in recent years another outlet—the op-ed page or column—has emerged. The opinion of the newspaper is usually expressed in unsigned editorials. Other articles appearing on the editorial page and opposite are presented to ensure a diversity of viewpoints. Op-ed columns are an expansion of the Letters to the Editor column. From the point of view of the newspaper the op-ed columns serve several purposes, explained Richard Cole, Dean of the School of Journalism, University of North Carolina. "First there is the public relations function, the value of the individual's name and his satisfaction at seeing his name in the paper and his piece of writing in the paper. Some newspapers even run little thumbnail pictures of the writers. It's good as a circulation builder for the newspaper. Helps the writer and readers feel they are part of the newspaper, too. Second, it permits a longer personal statement than the Letters to the Editor because these are usually kept short. A third reason is the essay might give a point of view that the newspaper has not thought about."

Suzanne Britt Jordan, who has published op-ed essays in *Newsweek*, *The New York Times*, the *Boston Globe*, and

Newsday, advises that you should go against the grain in your essay. "Take the most popular thing and slash it to pieces—that will sell! Write plainly, honestly, and with felicity. Phony-writing will get through to an editor. Work with the same old ideas but do them in a new way," says Jordan.

A postage stamp and some time writing your opinion for the Letters to the Editor column can bring the reward of seeing your own writing in print and gaining fast publication. In the case of a local community issue, let's say an application for a zoning change, someone may respond to your letter with support or disagreement on the subject. Before you know it a dialogue develops that may ultimately affect the decision of the local zoning board. Had you not voiced your views the zoning change may have passed without comment.

See also Book Reviewing

WRITING TIPS AND TECHNIQUES

In this section you will find a potpourri of tips on the techniques of writing that I have culled from various sources. Further information on the writing techniques that are used in Business and Trade Journal Writing, Fiction, Juvenile, News, and so on will be found in those sections.

The techniques of writing can be taught to almost anybody who wants to learn, Dean Richard Cole told me. "The techniques can be taught but the drive to write, the expression cannot. That must come from within." Doris Marston, a historical writer and lecturer concurs with Cole's opinion. She wrote to me: "A writer must know his own capability and decide whether he has the determination, even dedication, to do the work he has set out to do. He must overcome his fear of failure and be objective about his talents, at the same time. It is very helpful to the beginning writer to read the autobiographies of other writers to find the right perspective."

Writing talent does not develop itself; it must be nurtured. It requires action, dedication, planning, and goal setting. The goal of most writers is to see their work in print. Unfortunately, many are unsure of how to do this. Martha Monigle (The Florida Ghostwriter) observed that the reason inexperienced writers have trouble with their writing is because they don't set a distinct goal or purpose in each work. This causes ramblings, and repetition. If you find your writing wandering off from the original thread, Monigle suggests making a firm structure or outline even if this appears to be a mechanical contrivance. (See Formula For Features.)

"Thinking clearly is a conscious act that the writer must force upon himself just as if he were embarking on any other project that requires logic," wrote William Zinsser in *On Writing Well.* "Good writing doesn't come naturally, though most people obviously think it does. Good writing takes self discipline and, very often, self knowledge."

You must feel comfortable with your writing or it will not turn out successfully. As a writer you must ask yourself what interests you and then write about it. "Since few writers are successful in more than one field, you will save a great deal of time and effort by discovering early where your talents lie and by deciding in which particular field you wish to concentrate. . . .No matter which field you choose to labor in, you will be limited only by your talent and industry," wrote Isabelle Ziegler in *The Creative Writers' Handbook*.

In his book, *How To Write Stories That Sell*, Edward Fox encourages inexperienced writers to study the work of established authors. Fox points out the importance of reading similar material to the kind you want to write. "If you want to write for the magazines, read and study the magazines. If you want to be an historical novelist, read and study historical novels. If you want to be a mystery story writer, soak yourself in mystery stories. Look for the points of technique and see how the different authors have handled them." Fox, however, does not advocate the study of classical literature as a means of improving your own writing. "Styles in writing change from century to century. I seriously doubt if Dickens or Thackeray as new authors would be published today, even though they stand with the greats in literature," says Fox.

"Don't get it right; get it written," said Pete Ivey. While this advice may appear to be an invitation to slovenly writing the opposite is true, the intent is to help you get your work underway. Overcoming the initial inertia is a big challenge for writers most of the time. If you don't have a genuine deadline such as a "hurry up" call from an editor, set one for yourself.

Probably the biggest hurdle we all face is applying ourselves to the task of writing. Some people have trouble getting started because they doubt their own ability. They have a fear of failure and this prevents them from even making an attempt to write. Others find that although they have the time in which to write they are easily side-tracked. They sharpen pencils, tidy up their desk, even pay bills, do anything except get down to writing. And when they do eventually put a sheet of paper in the typewriter and want to get started the words refuse to come out. How can you prime the pump?

Start writing. If you must, advised one expert, write your name over and over. Just getting some words down on paper seems to break the mental roadblock. Keep in mind, every time you practice this kind of self control, there will be fewer roadblocks the next time; you'll do it easier. No matter how you get it down, don't try to compose final copy. Resign yourself to the fact that all you want is a rough draft. "Let your thoughts come out as though you we're conversing with your best friend," said Robert Clawson.

Don't stop to think about the form, revise it afterwards. David Lambuth's book, *The Golden Book on Writing*, explains why. "To stop to think about form in mid-career, while the idea is in motion, is like throwing out your clutch half-way up a hill and having to start in low again. You never get back to your old momentum."

Be prepared for loneliness. Shutting yourself away from other people is the only way to get those creative thoughts out of your head and down on paper. Let me share with you an excellent description of the loneliness of the writer. It appeared in John P. Marquand's *Wickford Point*, published by the Time Reading Program, 1966:

> ....It was a good a time as any other to start writing. . . .Until I actually faced it, I believed that it would not be difficult to write a short story, but now I recognized the complete loneliness of the trade as I stared at my blank paper. I was no longer dealing with facts. My mind was groping in the lamplight in an effort to draw the illusion of living people out of thin air. It had never occurred to me until that moment that the effort would be fatiguing or unpleasant; it had never occurred to me that it would be worse than manual labor. . . .
>
> ....I did not realize that writing would almost always be a disagreeable task, and that nothing which one sets down on paper ever wholly approximates the conception of the mind. As soon as I faced it, I did not want to write. Instead my intelligence presented a number of excuses for stopping before I started. The light was bad, the chair was uncomfortable; I felt tired; I wanted to read a book. I would always be seeking for excuses, ever after, not to write. . . .

Marquand's reflections on the task of writing raised another problem we frequently encounter, that of the dissatisfaction experienced when re-reading what we have written. Someone else's work always seems to be livelier, more descriptive, or more intelligent than our own. By comparison, our writing efforts appear to us to be weak shadows. Our minds may be overflowing with entertaining stories composed in rich, evocative phrases yet when we try to transfer them from the mind onto paper they evaporate or simply look dull. Woody Allen referred to this sense of dissatisfaction when he said: "When you write it, it gets less good because it never lives up to your original conception."

If you've been writing for a while and are constantly striving to improve your creative efforts, don't get discouraged. You should accept this feeling as a positive sign that you are changing from an amateur to a professional writer. A professional writer is an individual who is always striving to do better, who is never satisfied. He never stops to bask in the sun of past successes but, having reached a certain amount of success in one field, is willing to strike out anew in another.

Be ambitious; keep on writing and working out ways to improve your skill. Do not relax and accept less than the best for yourself and your readers. You have an obligation as a writer to give your readers the best ideas and words you are capable of producing.

The thought of having to communicate coherently on demand and on paper may seem to be insurmountable at the beginning of the creation of any story. Have heart that almost all writers go through this. Have heart, too, with the realization that all those articles that appear in so many magazines had writers that, at least for a little while, faced the identical problem.

The only way to become a writer is to write. In the words of my late friend, Pete Ivey: "When you have done your homework, reading, writing notes, setting it all down, and inspiration comes, you are ready to write. If inspiration doesn't come, you'd better start writing anyhow."

XEROX AND OTHER TRADE NAMES

Trade names and trademarks are considered to be valuable corporate assets. They make the product distinct, setting it apart from others of a similar nature. The last thing a corporation wants to see happen is that its unique trademark becomes adopted as the common name or generic term for products that may appear to be similar but are made by other companies.

Let's take the case of "XEROX." XEROX is both a trade name and a trademark. As a trade name it stands for the full corporate name "Xerox Corporation." As such the word Xerox may be used to refer to the Company itself or of the company such as Xerox headquarters, Xerox plans, or Xerox stock. Whenever used the word Xerox must always be capitalized.

The word "XEROX" as a registered trademark should be used only to identify XEROX products and services and to distinguish them from the products and services of others. Whenever you use the word XEROX, be sure that you are writing about the photocopy process or machine using xerography that is made by the Xerox Company and not some other. For example, IBM, Kodak, Nashua and Copystar all manufacture machines that make copies. In addition to the electrostatic method, copies may also be produced by machines utilizing heat, wet or dry processes, plates, pressure or stencils. The reason the Xerox Corporation is so protective of its trademark is that it does not want the word XEROX to become adopted, through misuse, as the popular name for a "copy."

Consider what happened to the trademark "Aspirin." It lost its uniqueness as a result of common use. Everybody started saying "aspirin" when they wanted a headache-relieving pill and pretty soon it was part of the language. Anybody who wanted to could make and market aspirin. Aspirin is not the only brand name to become popularized as a general noun. Kleenex, Frigidaire, Plexiglas, Mimeograph and

185

Escalator, are other proprietary products which have lost their identity by common use.

As writers we can help prevent the loss of a company's unique trademark by ensuring that we use it as a proper adjective and not as a possessive, or a verb. To write "we have many Xeroxes" would be incorrect. The same goes for "Xerox it." Instead, we should write, "make a Xerox copy of it."

Another company that is working hard to retain its trademark is the Caterpillar Tractor Company. You may have already seen its ads addressed directly to writers which explain that not all earth-moving equipment machines are CATERPILLARs[R]. "Other companies make products similar to ours and often paint theirs yellow, too. But they don't carry the CATERPILLAR name. . . .You can help sustain the meaning of our name by making sure you use our trademark only when you write about products we make."

As writers we ought to be fully aware of the importance of trademarks and copyrights. We do have an impact on the way words are used and misused. Let us protect the trust that others give us by making sure we use the correct words.

YOU SET THE PACE

The amount of time spent on writing or the pace at which the writer works varies according to each individual. The responses to the questionnaire that I sent out indicated that from two to six hours a day were spent on writing. Some writers work every day, others do not. With the exception of Dennis Hensley, who has an enviable record of sales and only spends two hours a night writing, almost all respondents said they write in the morning.

I'm also a morning worker when it comes to writing. Research and revisions are tasks that I tackle in the afternoon or evening. In the summer months my writing output drops, but I do more reading for pleasure during this period. This is the time when I read mysteries, science-fiction, and some of the classics that I never got around to reading before. The exposure to such different kinds of writing, quite unrelated to my field, turns out to be more than fun and relaxation. It also stimulates my creativity and vocabulary, while I can learn some new techniques.

Some people write slowly, some quickly. You must find out for yourself the pace that is best for you. Don't get concerned over speed, however, the main thing is to get started. In order to maintain a certain pace many writers set a writing quota of so many pages a day, or so many hours a day at their desk, rain or shine. If you are tackling a novel or non-fiction book this may be the only way to finish it. Sheila Hailey in *I Married A Best Seller*, said it takes her husband Arthur Hailey three years to write a book. Hailey's quota is 600 words a day, and he takes about six hours to do them. "Occasionally on a bad day when progress is slow, he will go back to his study after dinner to make up those 600 words." Hailey revises and rewrites as he goes along, the outcome being that when he nears the end of the book it really is the end. There isn't a massive rewrite job to be done.

Frederick Forsyth is another writer of best sellers who works on a page quota. Forsyth, author of the *Day of the*

187

Jackal, The Odessa File, and *Dogs of War,* sets himself the task of writing ten or twelve pages a day and starts work at 9 a.m. Typing on the same old and battered manual portable that he's been using for 20 years, as soon as he writes his quota he is up and away from his desk, even if it is only 11 a.m. In an interview with A. F. Gonzalez, Jr., Forsyth said, "I tried dictation but that was a disastrous experiment. I tried a dictating machine and burbled and chattered into it for about ten minutes and then played it back. . . .It was useless, and if transcribed by a typist it would have been meaningless."

Sidney Sheldon, author of *The Other Side of Midnight* and *Bloodline,* works at an even more impressive pace. Sheldon doesn't write rough drafts, he dictates them, reported interviewer Larry Holden. Sheldon dictates up to 50 pages a day, creating as he dictates. His first drafts are usually 1300-1500 pages. He then takes the transcribed pages and adds hand-written revisions on the front and back of each page. These pages are retyped and it's back to page one where he crosses out lines and adds more handwritten revisions. This process is repeated 12 to 15 times with Sheldon tightening up the manuscript on each revision.

It is well to write in the same place each day, because you become familiar with your surroundings and these automatically and habitually set up in you an urge to get to work. A change each day is apt to keep a writer off balance, said Edward Fox, *How to Write Stories That Sell.*

Creative isolation was a necessity for Richard McKenna, author of *The Sand Pebbles.* He said a knock on his door and the necessity to speak even a few words would dispel his writing mood. "A trip to the barbershop would destroy a whole day for me." McKenna's solution was to rent a room downtown, away from his home, and every morning before eight o'clock he would lock himself in with a Thermos of coffee and a sandwich. He would not come out of the room until after five o'clock. He did that seven days a week. McKenna was a writer who wrote only when he was in the mood. On days when he could not reach the writing mood he would do research for his stories; reading through science textbooks, making notes and stopping to reflect. Whatever he wrote when he was "in the mood," was better than when he tried to force the words, said McKenna.

By now you'll agree that to do a good job of writing you need to be able to concentrate. The fewer interruptions you have while writing the more likely you are to keep your chain of thought flowing. It is easy to prevent interruptions if you rent a room without a telephone and go there to write. Many writers dream of doing this and some can afford to carry it out. But what of the writer who has no alternative but to work at home? What if you have young children? This was my situation when I began my writing career. My daughters would leave for elementary school just after 8 a.m. and I would begin writing the moment they left. I tried to complete my writing stint before they returned home at 2:30 p.m. but some days, in an excess of enthusiasm and fervor for what I was doing, I would lose track of time.

One such day, I was typing at my desk, deep in concentration when both girls burst into the room noisily asking for this or that. I got very angry at being disturbed and pulled away from my thoughts, and shouted at them, "Leave me alone. Can't you see I'm busy! I'm writing a story of how parents can get along with their children."

They were startled into silence by my outburst and, as my words echoed in my head, I realized that before I could tell others how to solve their problems I was going to have to find a solution for mine. How could I get across to the children that although they could see me they were not to talk to me?

I thought about putting up a "Do Not Disturb" sign, but decided that they needed something even more visible, something that they could remember easily. I took a cotton cap that my husband used to wear when he was a Federal Meat Inspector and showed it to my daughters. It looked like a painter's cap with a bill. "Now, when you see me wearing this hat, it means I am thinking," I told them. "You must not disturb me, not even to say hello. I might be sitting at my typewriter, or I might be reading a book, but I'll be thinking and I won't want to be disturbed."

I explained to them the reason why I was going to wear the hat. "If you don't talk to me when I am working, you will be helping me to finish my work sooner and then I can spend some time with you," I said. "Of course, there are some times when you might have to interrupt me, and for those it will be all right. If there is an emergency, if you feel ill, or there's someone at the door for me then you may come and tell me." At first I think the girls thought it was a game. They may have thought it was funny to see me sitting at my desk wearing a cap, but they remembered it meant "Do Not Disturb," so it worked. I wore Ezra's cap for years, whenever I didn't want interruptions, and put it aside only a couple of years ago. In the end, the signal for my daughters turned out to be a signal for me. Whenever I put on my "writing cap" I knew that it was time to get down to work.

In the course of my writing years I have learned to pace myself. I no longer push myself to the point of fatigue and exhaustion in order to complete a story. I know that I get better results by working at a steady pace, so many hours a day, than by working eight hours one day and then slacking off the next. As a beginner in writing, the discipline, the work of writing takes time to develop. And this is to be expected. It is the doing of it, the practice of it, which gives the beginner the time for development of the art of writing. So, as Pete Ivey said, ". . .get it written."

See also Writing Tips

ZIP CODE

Always include the ZIP Code in the address to speed delivery of your mail. The ZIP Code system was introduced on July 1, 1963. It has been estimated that 92 percent of all first class mail now carries the 5-digit ZIP Code. The ZIP Code system divided the country into delivery units. Mail carrying a ZIP Code bypasses numerous handlings and goes directly to its destination. The Postal Service recently announced plans for adding four more digits to the 5-digit system. The program's timetable calls for adoption of the new system by 1981 and its use on a voluntary basis by 1983.

The U.S. Postal Service publishes the *National ZIP Code and Post Office Directory* annually. This is a two and a half inch thick publication, over 1,800 pages. Available by mail for $7.50 per copy from the Superintendent of Documents, U.S. Government Printing Office, Washington, D.C.20402.

Another useful directory is the *ZIP/Area Code Directory* available from Pilot Books, 347 Fifth Avenue, New York, NY 10016 at $2.95. per copy, postpaid. This directory relates the Postal ZIP Codes to the telephone system Area Codes and should be a great help and timesaver for those who are heavy telephone users. Assigned ZIP and Area Codes are listed by state with a numerical listing of Area Codes. If you have the ZIP Code of the person or business you want to call you can locate the Area Code in the directory. Then dial information directly (Area Code + 555 1212) for the number you want. Alternatively, if you have the address and phone number but no Area Code, you can find the code quickly without operator assistance.

LIST OF REFERENCES

Adams, John B. Professor, School of Journalism, University of North Carolina, Chapel Hill, NC. Personal interview April 1980.

Angione, Howard, Editor. *The Associated Press Stylebook and Libel Manual.* The Associated Press, NY. 1977.

Ashley, Paul P. *Say It Safely.* University of Washington Press, 3rd Edition, Seattle, WA. 1966.

Barzun, Jacques, and Henry F. Graff. *The Modern Researcher.* Harcourt Brace Jovanovich, Inc., 3rd Edition, NY. 1977.

Campbell, Walter S. *Writing: Advice and Devices.* Doubleday & Co., NY. 1950.

Casewit, Curtis. *Freelance Writing.* Macmillan Publishing Co., NY. 1974.

Clawson, Robert. Instructor, Technocopy, Inc., Communications Course, 31 South Street, Morristown, NY 07960.

Cole, Richard R. Dean, School of Journalism, University of North Carolina, Chapel Hill, NY. Personal interview May 1980.

Copperud, Roy H. *American Usage and Style: The Consensus.* Van Nostrand Reinhold Co. NY. 1980.

Copyright Office. *Application for Copyright Registration.* Form TX. U.S. Government Printing Office, Washington, DC.

Copyright Office. *Copyright Fees Effective January 1, 1978.* Circular R4. U.S. Government Printing Office, Washington, DC.

Copyright Office. *Deposit of Copies Without Accompanying Application.* Circular R7a. U.S. Government Printing Office, Washington, DC.

Copyright Office. *Highlights of the New Copyright Law.* Circular R99. U.S. Government Printing Office, Washington, DC.

Copyright Office, *New Classification System for Copyright Registrations.* Circular R1c. U.S. Government Printing Office. Washington, DC.

Copyright Office. *New Copyright Registration Procedures.* Circular R1d. U.S. Government Printing Office, Washington, DC.

Deal, Borden. "Letter to a Son Who Has Declared His Ambition to Become a Writer," *The Writer*, November 1974.

Explore, Explain, Expand. Publicity Handbook published by the North Carolina Triangle Chapter, Women in Communications, Inc. 1974.

Felber, Stanley B., and Arthur Hoch. *What Did You Say?* Prentice-Hall, Inc., NJ. 1973.

Fox, Edward S. *How to Write Stories That Sell.* The Writer, Inc., Boston, MA. 1961.

Giles, Carl H. *Writing Right To Sell.* A. B. Barnes & Co., Inc., NJ. 1970.

Glassman, Don. *Writers' & Artists' Rights.* Writers Press, Washington, DC. 1978.

Goeller, Carl. *Writing to Communicate.* Doubleday & Co., NY. 1974.

Greisman, Bernard, Editor. *J. K. Lasser's Your Income Tax*, Simon and Schuster, NY. 1980.

Hilliard, Celia. "A Quick Review of the Basics of Reviewing," *Writer's Digest*, May 1975.

Henry, Omer. "Increase Your Article Sales," *The Writer*, April 1975.

Holmes, Marjorie, *Writing the Creative Article*, The Writer, Boston, MA. 1973.

Hutchinson, Lois I. *Standard Handbook for Secretaries*, McGraw-Hill Co., NY. 1972.

Instant Quotation Dictionary. Donald O. Bolander, and others. Career Institute, Mundelein, IL. 1969.

Jacobs, Hayes B. *Writing and Selling Non-Fiction.* Writer's Digest, OH. 1967.

Kerns, Robert L. *Photojournalism: Photography With A Purpose.* Prentice-Hall, Inc., NJ. 1980.

Lambuth, David, and others. *The Golden Book on Writing.* The Viking Press, NY. 1964.

Longo, Lucas. "Book Reviewing," *The Writer*, July 1975.

Marquand, John P. *Wickford Point.* Time Reading Program, NY. 1966.

Mathieu, Aron M., Editor. *The Creative Writer.* Writer's Digest. 2nd Revised Edition. Ohio. 1972.

McKenna, Richard. *New Eyes for Old*. John F. Blair. NC. 1972.

McLarn, Jack Clinton. *Writing Part-time for Fun and Money*. Enterprise Publishing Co., Delaware. 1978.

Nordland, Rod. *Names and Numbers: A Journalist's Guide to the Most Needed Information Sources and Contacts*. John Wiley & Sons, NY. 1978.

Oleksy, Walter G. *1,000 Tested Money-making Markets for Writers*. Barnes & Noble, NY. 1974.

Polking, Kirk., and Leonard S. Meranus, Editors. *Law and the Writer*. Writer's Digest, OH. 1978.

Presson, Hazel. *Interviewing*. Richards Rosen Press, Inc., NY. 1979.

Reynolds, Paul R. "Getting an Agent," *The Writer*. October 1972.

Ruark, Robert C. *The Honey Badger*. Fawcett Publications, Inc., Conn. 1965.

Schapper, Beatrice, Editor. *Writing the Magazine Article*. Writer's Digest, OH. 1970.

Sissman, L. E. "Book Reviewing," *The Writer*, October 1974.

Skillin, Marjorie E., Robert M. Gay and others. *Words Into Type*, Prentice-Hall, Inc., 3rd edition, NJ. 1974.

Strunk, William, Jr. and E. B. White. *The Elements of Style*, The Macmillan Co., NY. 1959.

Wainwright, David. *Journalism Made Simple*, W. H. Allen & Co., London. 1972.

Weisinger, Mort. "Titles That Talk," *The Writer*, August 1975.

Williamson, Daniel R. *Feature Writing for Newspapers*, Communications Arts Books, Hastings House, 2nd Printing, NY. 1977.

Writers' & Artists' Year Book. Adam and Charles Black, London. 1976.

Writer's Market. William Brohaugh, Editor. Writer's Digest Books, OH. 1980.

Yolen, Jane. *Writing Books for Children*. The Writer, Inc. MA. 1973.

Zeigler, Isabelle. *The Creative Writer's Handbook*. Barnes & Noble, NY. 1975.

Zinsser, William. *On Writing Well: An Informal Guide to Writing of Nonfiction*. Harper & Row, NY. 1976.

INDEX

Vacation Homes
—on land or sea

Weymouth
On Creative

BY RITA BERMAN

"What separates writers from all other artists is that writers don't really want to write," Coates Redmon suggested in an

Renting a house by the sea is very popular with American families, particularly if they have school-age children. Faced with the prospect of a 10-week summer vacation, cooped up in an air-conditioned house with children who complain, "There's nothing to do, and it's too hot to play outside," many families either send their children away to summer camp, or rent a house by the sea. On weekends father takes a break from work and comes to join them.

On the East Coast, for example, from June to the end of August, families from New York, New Jersey, Virginia and Maryland travel to North Carolina to vacation in a rented house or duplex apartment right on the beach. The North Carolina coast offers a wonderful combination of sandy beaches and dune, waterways and sounds, old sea-ports a~

Photo by Ezra Ber

SHELLING

By Rita Berman

As a recreation, shell collecting has ancient roots. The Romans collected shells as playthings for the leisured class. During the Renaissance period shells were treasured collector's items in Europe. It wasn't until the late seventeenth century when the first illustrated shell books were published that the was opened for a wider

Growing Older
Affects Us A

Rita Berman

[Mrs. Berman, a free-la writer, contributes reg to the Times-Outlook.

It has been said that only wine cheese benefit from aging; but wh about man? Aging, after all, is no disease but a normal and natural b process in which we constantly ur go change physically, physiologic and psychologically. Included in psychological changes are our reli